Ava's Dream

Joseph J. Ridgway

DEDICATION

FOR:

My wife, Diane, who showed me how love and friendship are two sides of the same coin of gold;

My father, who taught me equity and accountability;

My mother, who taught me empathy;

My children, who taught me that life is not a straight line;

My grandchildren, who daily remind me of the gifts of youth and hope;

My grandparents, who gave me unconditional love and taught me the value of sacrifice;

and,

The children of the world, wherever and whoever they are, because they will decide the future of humanity.

INTRODUCTION

Welcome, all readers, and thank you for allowing me to share with you an important part of the amazing story of our United States Constitution. *Ava's Dream* travels beyond the unbelievable and well-known tale of our Founding Fathers who risked their careers, their families, and their own lives to start a new country by revolting against the awesome power of Great Britain and its ruler, King George III. We all know our revolution was successful; what followed, however, truly was the most incredible part of our history.

Think of sitting at your desk while attempting to write a plan the government and people of our new country will follow forever, a plan that would provide the means to justice and freedom for all, which were previously denied. What would you write? How would you begin?

Our Founding Fathers decided to start with these three words, "We the People..." Clearly, they were saying we wanted to govern ourselves. For almost 250 years, we have done just that: we have governed ourselves. Governance has not been perfect - no human is. While sometimes taking two steps forward and one step back, we continuously persevere.

What has been the single most important key to our success? How have we been able to keep on the path of self-governance without finding ourselves lost in the woods? My hope is the tale told in this book answers, in large part, these questions. It is also my wish that the readers, many of whom are the future safe-keepers of our nation, will remember the importance of this lesson as you continue on your path as one of "We the People."

~ Joseph Ridgway

TABLE OF CONTENTS

CHAPTER ONE

The Dream

Ava had always been an inquisitive, compassionate child. The year was 1953, and it was early in the morning on a cool day in late June. Ava had just woken from a strange and mysterious overnight dream. Her immediate remembrance was cloudy and obscure. Even though she could only recall scant fragments of her dream, the parts Ava did remember were clear and vivid. Curiously, the dream felt very important, even fateful. But she couldn't understand or guess why.

In Ava's dream, there were many strangers—people she had never seen before, each one different in appearance. Some were tall, others short; some had dark hair, while others had hair as white as snow. They wore clothes that seemed from different times and places, but all of them had one thing in common: they were all staring directly at her. Their eyes were filled with a mix of curiosity and hope, as if they were waiting for her to speak, to give them the answers they desperately needed. But Ava was just an 11-year-old girl, and she couldn't begin to understand what these strangers might want from her. It was as if they believed she held some great secret or knowledge, but the truth was, Ava had no idea what that could be.

The dream didn't scare her, but it left her feeling uneasy and confused. As she slowly woke up, the images of the strangers began to fade, but the feeling of being watched, of being expected to know something important, lingered. She tried to push the strange thoughts out of her mind, focusing instead on the exciting day that lay ahead. After all, there were things to do and places to be, and she didn't want to start the day feeling unsettled.

But the dream wouldn't leave her alone. Throughout the day, and in the days that followed, Ava kept seeing brief flashes of the dream. It was as if her mind was replaying bits and pieces of it, trying to remind her of something she had forgotten. These flashbacks would come at the most unexpected times—while she was playing, reading, or even when she was talking to her friends. The images of the strangers, with their expectant eyes, kept returning, and Ava couldn't shake the feeling that the dream was trying to tell her something important. It was as though the dream held a message, a lesson she needed to learn, even if she didn't yet understand what that lesson was.

The flash-backs were in the form of expressions of thoughts seemingly related to the people she saw in her dream. For example, there were voiceless utterances such as *It doesn't matter if you are a boy or a girl. It doesn't matter what color skin you have. It doesn't matter if you are rich or poor. It doesn't matter if you are sick or well. It doesn't matter where you were born or where you now live. It doesn't matter which God hears your prayers. It doesn't matter whether you are loud or quiet or whether you are happy or sad. It doesn't matter if you were adopted. It doesn't matter whether you have a mother, father, stepmother, or stepfather. Nor does it matter how many grandfathers or grandmothers you have. It doesn't matter how many uncles, aunts, and cousins you have. Nor does it matter how many brothers and sisters you have or whether you are the only child in your family. It doesn't matter whether you are short, tall, slim or plump, young or old. It doesn't matter what color hair you have or whether it is short, long, straight, or curly. It doesn't even matter whether you have any hair at all.*

After much contemplation, Ava gained a stronger sense of the once vague and unspoken idea or feeling for what seemed to be the dream's lesson: *The only thing that matters is how much you care about others, regardless of their differences, and how far you are willing to go to help them.*

CHAPTER TWO

Ava Isabella and the Playground Park

Ava's middle name was Isabella, and she possessed great beauty. Her beauty was not a result of being pretty in the conventional sense, however. It resulted from her authenticity and honesty. Her beauty did not originate from her outward appearance but rather from her heart and mind. Because Ava Isabella's beauty was sincere and true, it would never fade or disappear in the face of sickness or even old age.

Ava had just recently turned 11 years old, and this particular day was one she had been eagerly anticipating for what felt like forever. Her excitement was bubbling over, filling her with a sense of thrill and energy, yet there was also a tiny flicker of nervousness deep in her stomach. It was as though a swarm of happy, fluttering butterflies had taken up residence there, their wings creating a mix of excitement and a hint of unease. This feeling wasn't because the school year had just ended—Ava actually enjoyed school and didn't mind it ending—but rather because something far more exciting was happening in her town. The brand-new playground park, which everyone had been talking about for months, was finally opening, and the whole town was buzzing with excitement.

For as long as Ava could remember, the entire town had been impatiently counting down the days until the school year ended and the park's gates would open wide to welcome everyone. During the cold, snowy winter and the blossoming spring, Ava had seen the bright, colorful posters announcing the park's opening everywhere she went. They were on every tree, every telephone pole, each one more vibrant and inviting than the last, promising endless fun and adventure. Ava would stop and stare at them, imagining all the fun she would have once the park was open.

And now, the wait was over. The trucks, construction equipment, and busy workers who had been there for so long were finally gone, leaving behind only the promise of excitement and joy. Ava, along with her family and friends, was more than ready to step into this new world of fun. She had been dreaming about this day for so long that she could barely contain her excitement. The large silver double gates that marked the entrance to the park seemed to gleam in the sunlight, almost as if they were inviting her in. Ava could hardly wait to push those gates open and step into the park. She imagined the thrill of playing on the rides, the joy of splashing in the sparkling pools, and the delight of wandering along the winding paths, discovering new adventures at every turn. But what excited her most was the thought of exploring the park's many trees, each one offering shade and beauty, and the endless array of flowers, bursting with colors and fragrances that filled the air with a sweet, joyful scent.

Ava could barely stand still, her heart racing with the anticipation of all the fun that awaited her. The park was no longer just a dream or a picture on a poster; it was real, and it was finally here. She knew that this day would be one to remember for a long, long time.

Ava was in such good spirits she actually allowed her mother to help choose her outfit for the big day. She wanted to look her best but still wanted to wear play-clothes to take full advantage of the park's many outdoor features. After accepting her mother's fashion advice, she chose green shorts, a white top, and her new orange sneakers. Ava was finally ready to go. She grabbed her bathing suit and towel, snatched the book she was reading from her night-stand, and ran to jump into her mother's car.

As Ava's mother searched for a parking space, Ava became unusually quiet and couldn't stop staring out of the car's windows at the fanfare. The town had lavishly decorated the exterior of the park with red, white, and blue crepe paper, along with balloons of many different colors, shapes, and sizes.

Upon stepping through its large silver gates at the park's entrance, Ava and her mother noticed many of the balloons were in the shapes of different animals and were affixed to trees, park benches, and even the rides themselves. There were bright red and gold swings, yellow monkey bars, purple seesaws, and long orange sliding boards. There were spacious sandboxes, wooden forts, brown and white tree houses, and five carousels of different colors. There were volley-ball nets, aswell as basketball and tennis courts. There was also a gigantic pale blue swimming pool, with several separate smaller pools for people of varying ages and abilities. Ava's impression of the park greatly exceeded even her lofty expectations.

The park wasn't just a place for running, playing, and splashing in the pools; it was also a haven for those who wanted to relax and enjoy some quiet time. Scattered throughout the park were numerous cozy seating areas, each one thoughtfully designed to offer peace and tranquility. These inviting spots were nestled under the shade of tall, leafy trees, and surrounded by colorful flower beds bursting with vibrant hues. The flowers' sweet fragrances filled the air, creating a perfect atmosphere for reading a good book, daydreaming, or simply sitting back and soaking in the beauty of nature. Ava could imagine herself curling up on one of the benches with her favorite book, lost in a story while the gentle rustle of leaves and the distant sound of laughter filled the background.

One of Ava's favorite discoveries was a special area dedicated entirely to reading and writing. This section of the park was surrounded by an array of intricately shaped topiaries, each one crafted to resemble different animals and fantastical creatures. The carefully trimmed greenery gave the space a magical feel, almost as if Ava was in the company of silent, leafy friends who watched over her as she let her imagination run wild. It was a place where stories came to life, where ideas flowed freely, and where the simple act of putting pen to paper felt like a grand adventure.

As Ava explored further, she noticed three shiny green water fountains, their cool, clear water sparkling in the sunlight. These fountains were a thoughtful addition, perfect for quenching the thirst of anyone who needed a refreshing drink on a hot summer day. Ava could already picture herself running to one of them after a long day of play, the cold water a welcome relief. Nearby, she spotted three more fountains that looked just like the first ones, but these were shorter, carefully designed so that even the smallest children could easily reach them. The park had truly thought of everything, ensuring that every visitor, no matter how young or old, felt welcome and cared for.

Ava couldn't have asked for a more perfect day. The park was everything she had imagined and more. She spent hours playing with her friends, laughing and enjoying the many wonders the park had to offer. Families gathered together, sharing in the joy of the day, from toddlers toddling along the paths to grandparents relaxing in the shade. It was clear that this park was built for everyone, a place where all ages could come together and find something special just for them.

As the day drew to a close, Ava knew one thing for certain: she would be coming back to this park as often as she could. It had been worth every moment of waiting, and she couldn't wait to return to discover even more of its magic.

CHAPTER THREE

Sofia Jo and Her Dog Sadie

O ne day, as Ava was walking toward the park entrance after being dropped off by her mother, she spied on her friend Sofia Jo. Sofia Jo was sitting with her father in the front seat of their car, which was parked just outside the silver entrance gates to the park.

Sofia Jo had been born blind. Because of that circumstance, she was always accompanied by her seeing-eye dog, whose name was Sadie. Sadie was a service dog who was trained to help people with disabilities like Sofia Jo. Sadie helped guide Sofia Jo wherever the little girl went, staying by her side and helping her by taking the place of her unseeing eyes. Sadie was a friendly dog and loved all of Sofia Jo's friends, including Ava. The children all loved to pet Sadie and wanted to scratch behind her ears, but they understood sometimes it was best to leave Sadie to attend to the dog's duties - working to take care of and protect Sofia Jo.

Before stepping through the gates of the park, Ava noticed something that made her pause. She saw her friend Sofia Jo sitting in the front seat of her family's car, with her loyal dog Sadie by her side. Sofia Jo's father was in the driver's seat, looking as if he were waiting for something. Ava's heart leapt with excitement at the thought of spending the day at the park with her dear friend, so she hurried over to the car, her smile bright and eager.

"Hey, Sofia Jo!" Ava called out as she reached the car. "Do you and Sadie want to come with me into the park and play together?" She could already imagine the fun they'd have, exploring the playground, splashing in the pool, and running through the open spaces. But as she waited for Sofia Jo's reply, something in her friend's expression made Ava's smile falter.

Sofia Jo turned her head slightly away, trying to hide the tears that began to fill her eyes. She shook her head sadly, the movement slow and heavy, as if each shake brought more heartache. Ava noticed how Sofia Jo's hand reached out to gently stroke Sadie's fur, seeking comfort in her dog's familiar presence. Confused, Ava looked to Sofia Jo's father, hoping for an explanation.

"I don't understand," Ava said, her voice filled with concern and confusion. Why wouldn't Sofia Jo want to join her on such an exciting day?

Sofia Jo's father sighed deeply, his face a mix of disappointment and helplessness. He pointed to a large white sign with bold black letters that stood near the entrance to the park. Ava followed his gaze and read the sign: 'NO DOGS ALLOWED IN THE PARK.' The words seemed to jump out at her, stark and unyielding.

"Because Sofia Jo needs Sadie to guide her and keep her safe, she can't go into the park," Sofia Jo's father explained gently, though his voice was tinged with sadness. "Sadie isn't allowed inside, so neither is Sofia Jo."

Ava's heart sank as the realization hit her. The very park they had all been so excited about was now a source of sorrow for her friend. The sign was just a few simple words, but its impact was profound. Ava felt a deep sense of unfairness welling up inside her, seeing how something so wonderful could turn into something so disappointing for Sofia Jo. She looked at her friend, who was trying her best to be brave, but the tears that slipped down her cheeks told Ava everything she needed to know. This day, which should have been filled with joy, was now clouded by an unexpected and painful barrier.

CHAPTER FOUR

Pop-Pop

That evening, Ava's grandfather came to dinner with Ava and her family at their home. Her grandfather's name was Zachary Joseph. His friends sometimes called him 'ZJ,' but to Ava, he was simply 'Pop-Pop.' They had a special relationship which lucky grandparents and their grandchildren very often enjoy.

Ava was absolutely delighted with her grandfather, whom she affectionately called Pop-Pop, and she cherished the special bond they shared. The connection between them was unlike anything else in her life—a blend of deep love, mutual respect, and an unspoken understanding that seemed to tie their hearts together in a unique way. Ava knew that no matter what, she could always count on Pop-Pop to be there for her, and the feeling was more precious to her than anything.

Years ago, when Ava was only two years old, a tragedy had struck their family. Her father, a brave pilot, had lost his life when the B-25 Bomber he was flying crashed on the island of Iwo Jima, near the end of World War II. Although Ava was too young to remember him, she had grown up hearing stories about her father's courage and the love he had for his family. His loss had left a void that was impossible to fill, but it was her grandfather—her father's father—who had stepped into that empty space with all the love and dedication he had. He became both a father and a grandfather to Ava, a role he embraced fully, showering her with affection, wisdom, and the steady presence she needed.

Ava's mother never remarried, choosing instead to focus all her love and attention on raising her daughter. This meant that Ava grew up as an only child, but she was never lonely. Her grandfather made sure of that. Pop-Pop filled her life with laughter, stories, and the kind of guidance that only someone with his life experience could offer. Ava highly respected him—not just because he was her grandfather, but because of the kind of person he was. He was kind, thoughtful, and always seemed to know what to do or say, no matter the situation.

Pop-Pop had a wonderful sense of humor that could brighten even the darkest days. He was always ready with a joke or a funny story that would leave Ava giggling uncontrollably. But beyond his humor, there was a deep intelligence that Ava admired greatly. Her mother had told her that Pop-Pop was a lawyer, a person who had spent many years in school learning how to help people solve their problems. This fact made Ava proud. She loved knowing that her grandfather used his knowledge to make a difference in the world, helping those in need with his sharp mind and big heart.

To Ava, Pop-Pop was more than just a grandfather—he was a hero, a role model, and the most important person in her life. Their relationship was a constant source of joy and comfort, something that Ava knew she would treasure forever.

Knowing these things about Pop-Pop presented Ava with an idea. She revealed Sofia Jo's problem to her grandfather. She spelled out how Sofia Jo couldn't experience the park because her seeing-eye dog Sadie was not allowed inside. Ava explained that because Sofia Jo was blind, she needed Sadie to guide her and keep her safe by being her eyes. This made Ava very frustrated, and she felt that it was unfair for her and her other friends to enjoy the park while Sofia Jo was excluded. "Do you think you can help Sofia Jo with her problem, Pop-Pop?" she asked with overwhelming concern. Her grandfather looked at Ava, and he sensed her hope and trust in him.

He was very proud that Ava was concerned about her friend and even more pleased that she wanted to help. He told Ava that he would think about Sofia Jo's problem and would return the following weekend so they could work together on trying to possibly help her. Ava was very happy, as well as hopeful. She didn't mind skipping her trip to the park and staying home with her grandfather to work on a plan. In any event, it was difficult for Ava to fully enjoy the park when she knew that Sofia Jo was being left out.

Ava could hardly wait for the weekend. Saturday morning finally arrived, and so did her grandfather. "Are you ready to get to work?" he asked. Ava's answering smile revealed her agreement and joy.

Ava and her grandfather began to discuss Sofia Jo's problem and what could be done to solve it. First, her grandfather explained that the words on the sign, 'NO DOGS ALLOWED IN THE PARK,' was a law or rule which must be obeyed by everyone. "But what if a law is a bad law? Must a bad law also be obeyed?" Ava asked.

"Those are very good questions," her grandfather replied. "But who gets to decide which laws are good and which laws are bad?" he asked. "What would happen if everyone only obeyed the laws they thought were good and disobeyed the laws they thought were bad? Wouldn't the result be the same as having no laws?"

"I don't understand," said Ava.

"Let me give you an example," said her grandfather. He paused for a moment and then asked Ava to repeat for him a rule that her school required everyone to obey.

Ava thought and thought and suddenly brightened. "I have one," she said. "NO RUNNING DURING FIRE DRILLS."

"That *is* a good example," said her grandfather. "Do you think that is a good rule or a bad rule?" he asked.

"That's a good rule, of course," Ava answered immediately.

"And why do you believe it to be a good rule, Ava?" asked her grandfather.

"Because I learned in school that if students start running at the sound of the fire alarm, they may fall and hurt themselves or others at a time when they need to remain calm," she confidently answered.

Her grandfather looked at her and asked, "But what if I thought it was a bad rule because running would get me out of the building and away from the fire faster? We all know that running is faster than walking. And what would happen if each person could choose to obey or disobey the 'No Running' rule? You would then have some people running and others walking. That would be the same as having no rule."

"But what does this have to do with Sofia Jo's problem?" asked Ava.

Pop-Pop looked at Ava thoughtfully. "Why do you think the law does not allow dogs in the park?" he asked.

"I don't know," said Ava.

"Why don't we think of some possible reasons," he said. "One reason might be that dogs go to the bathroom on the ground, and this is unclean. Adults and children could step or fall in dog excrement. Other reasons might include the following: some dogs are not friendly to children or strangers, and they could possibly bite or scratch someone; some dogs are very small and could accidentally trip someone; some dogs are very large and could accidentally knock someone over; some dogs don't get along with other dogs, and they could fight with each other which could be dangerous; some adults and children are simply afraid of dogs and would not be able to visit the park because of their fear."

Ava's grandfather then looked at her very seriously, "Aren't these examples good reasons for not allowing dogs in the park?" Ava looked doubtful, but she had to nod in agreement.

"Does that mean it is a good law because it was written for good reasons?" she asked.

"That is another very good question, and I would generally have to answer yes," her grandfather responded. Ava looked downcast.

"Does that mean there is nothing we can do because it is a good law?" Ava worriedly asked. Her grandfather smiled. "Sometimes, even good laws can turn into bad laws if they treat people unfairly or unequally," he answered. Now, it was Ava's turn to smile. "I will see you tomorrow and we'll continue our discussion," he answered, while returning her smile.

CHAPTER FIVE

A Civics Lesson

The next day, as Ava opened the door for her grandfather, she sensed that he had an idea to help Sofia Jo, but didn't yet know specifically what he had in mind. "So what can we do, Pop-Pop?" Ava immediately asked. "First," her grandfather began, "I want to teach you a quick civics lesson. You will learn much more about it from your teachers in school as you get older."

"Civics?" she asked while frowning.

"Yes. Civics is a subject of learning, like history, reading, writing, mathematics and other subjects. It is actually the study of the rights and duties of citizens and how our government works," he explained.

"Why is that important for me to learn right now?" Ava asked.

Ava's grandfather thought a moment and asked, "Isn't Sofia Jo a citizen of our town? In other words, doesn't Sofia Jo live in our town and go to school here?"

"Yes," said Ava.

"And don't you believe that Sofia Jo should have the right to go to the park like everyone else?"

"Of course I do," answered Ava.

"Then we must look to the subject of civics to learn how we might be able to solve Sofia Jo's problem," he responded.

"This won't take the rest of your life to learn, but you will remember it for the rest of your life. You will be able to use your brain to help your friend. Civics is a critical ingredient of my legal education and profession as a lawyer, but it should be learned by every citizen. Are you still willing and interested in helping Sofia Jo?" he asked.

"Yes, I'm very interested," answered Ava.

"Sometimes helping others requires learning and thinking about subjects, ideas, and questions in ways you have never thought about before," said her grandfather.

"In what ways?" she asked.

"For instance," continued her grandfather, "who wrote the law that reads 'NO DOGS ALLOWED IN THE PARK?' Why was the law written? Who determines whether it's a good law or a bad law? How do you get rid of a bad law? And who do you seek out in order to change a bad law? These are just some of the questions we'll need to answer in order to help Sofia Jo."

"Will you help me answer those questions, Pop-Pop?" asked Ava. "Yes, I will," said her grandfather. "But it will take a persistent effort on both of our parts to be successful." Ava slowly nodded in uncertain agreement.

"Before we start, I think we should have some lemonade and cookies," he pleasantly suggested. Ava readily agreed and went to the kitchen and returned with two large glasses of cold lemonade and a plate of cookies for her grandfather, who had already taken a seat on Ava's front porch. It was fun for Ava to have her grandfather as her teacher, and she tried very hard to understand his lessons. She wanted to learn what her grandfather did as a lawyer, especially because they were working together to help her friend Sofia Jo.

After taking a few sips of their drinks and more than a few cookies, her grandfather started to instruct Ava. "Our government has three parts or branches," he said. "Think of our government as a tree with three branches. Do you remember me asking you who wrote the law not allowing dogs in the park?" "Yes, I do," answered Ava.

"The answer is that the legislature of our town wrote the law," he said.

"What is the legislature?" she asked. "The legislature is a group of citizens who were elected by the vote of the people to write our laws," Pop-Pop continued.

"You can think of laws as rules or regulations which are written to govern or control our conduct which everyone must follow and obey, such as the speed limit and stop signs which appear on our roadways. This part of our government is called the legislative branch. As I said earlier, those in the legislature were elected by the citizens of our town, like your mother and your father, when he was alive. Your teachers, police officers, fire persons, and other citizens all voted in the election, including me!" he laughingly added. "When you get older, you will also be able to vote for whomever you choose to elect as a member of the legislature. You will learn people have different opinions about which ideas would result in good or bad laws. Ava, do you understand how important it is for you to vote for honorable people because those elected to the legislature have the job of writing our laws?" he asked.

"Yes, I believe so," said Ava, narrowing her eyes in concentration.

"Do you remember when I asked you why the law not allowing dogs in the park was written?" said her grandfather.

"Yes, I do," said Ava.

"And do you remember agreeing that the law was probably written for many good reasons?" he asked.

"Yes," replied Ava. "But Pop-Pop, I still think the law is unfair."

"I understand," said her grandfather, "and we will eventually get to that. Just have a little patience."

Ava trusted her grandfather and she also loved learning, so she took another cookie and again sat back to listen as he continued his lesson.

"The second part or branch of our government is called the executive branch. This part enforces the laws which were written by the legislative branch. For example, if Sofia Jo decided to disobey the law and tried to enter the park with Sadie, the park policeman would be required to stop and prevent her from entering the park. It is the policeman's job to make sure that everyone obeys the law. This is part of the role and job of the executive branch of our government," he explained.

After taking another sip of lemonade, he looked at Ava and continued. "The third part or branch of our government is called the judicial branch. The role and job of the judicial branch is to explain and interpret what the laws mean and to make sure that our laws do not treat people differently from each other without a justifiable reason."

"These three parts of our government were created by the United States Constitution, which is the supreme law of our entire country, including our town," he said. "Our state also has its own constitution, which is very similar to our country's Constitution," Pop-Pop added. "A constitution is a written law which sets forth the laws of a nation, or a state, and determines the powers and duties of the government, as well as guaranteeing certain rights to the people living there," he explained.

Ava was listening closely, her eyes fixed on her grandfather as he spoke. She was trying hard to understand everything he was saying about the three branches of government. But at the same time, her mind kept drifting back to Sofia Jo and her dog, Sadie. How could these branches of government—things that seemed so big and far away—help them solve the problem? All Ava wanted was for Sofia Jo and Sadie to be allowed into the park, just like everyone else. But the more she thought about it, the more complicated it seemed.

As these thoughts filled her mind, Ava noticed that her grandfather had suddenly grown quiet. His voice, which had been explaining everything so patiently, had stopped. Ava glanced up at him, wondering what he was thinking about. She didn't want to interrupt him, so she sat quietly, waiting for him to speak again.

But the silence stretched on. It felt like a very long time, and Ava started to worry. Her grandfather was usually so full of ideas—what if he couldn't think of a plan to help Sofia Jo? What if this time, there wasn't an answer? The thought made Ava's heart sink a little. She looked at her grandfather, hoping that any moment now, he would come up with one of his great ideas, the kind that always made her feel better.

CHAPTER SIX

The Policeman

"**I** believe I have an idea about how we can best utilize the three branches of our government to help Sofia Jo," announced Ava's grandfather. "Do you remember what I taught you regarding the three branches?" he asked.

"Yes," said Ava, although she couldn't remember their names. "First, we will approach the executive branch," he said.

"How do we do that?" Ava asked. "Come with me," said her grandfather. "Where are we going?"

"We are going to the park!" he exclaimed.

As they drove to the park, Pop-Pop explained to Ava the park policeman was part of the executive branch and that he would be their starting point. When they arrived at the park, Ava's grandfather realized they were in luck.

The park policeman was standing at the park's entrance directly next to the sign that read 'NO DOGS ALLOWED IN THE PARK.' Ava and her grandfather got out of the car and approached the policeman. "Good day, sir," said her grandfather to the policeman.

"And good day to you as well," answered the officer.

Ava's grandfather gently placed a hand on her shoulder as they approached the park entrance where the policeman stood. With a warm smile, he introduced Ava to the officer, who bent down slightly to be at Ava's eye level. In a friendly tone, the policeman asked, "Did you come to the park today to play and enjoy this beautiful weather?" His voice was cheerful, and his eyes twinkled as he spoke, as if he was already picturing Ava having fun on the swings or running around with her friends.

But instead of nodding eagerly as she usually would, Ava simply shook her head no. Her excitement about the park had faded, replaced by the serious matter that had brought her here today. She glanced up at her grandfather, silently seeking his support.

The policeman, noticing Ava's unusual quietness, straightened up and looked back at her grandfather, curiosity now replacing his earlier smile. He could tell there was something more going on. Ava's grandfather, sensing the officer's curiosity, took a deep breath and explained why they were really there. "We didn't come to the park to play today," he began gently. "We actually wanted to talk to you about the 'NO DOGS ALLOWED IN THE PARK' sign."

The policeman's friendly expression turned thoughtful as he listened, realizing that this was no ordinary visit. He could see that Ava and her grandfather had something important on their minds.

"Sure. What about it?" the policeman asked.

With that, the three of them sat down on one of the park's exterior perimeter benches. Ava was nervous but determined to help her friend. At her grandfather's urging, she told the policeman about Sofia Jo's problem. She told him how her friend was blind and couldn't play in the park because her seeing-eye service dog, Sadie, wasn't permitted in the park. Ava explained how Sofia Jo needed Sadie to be her eyes, guide her, and keep her safe while she enjoyed the park with the rest of her friends. "Can you help her?" she asked. As the policeman thought about what was asked of him, Ava silently wondered whether he would let Sofia Jo and Sadie in the park because, as she believed, the law on the sign was unfair to Sofia Jo.

The officer felt bad for both Ava and Sofia Jo. However, he explained his job was to enforce the law and to make sure that everyone obeys the law, whether he personally felt it was fair. He couldn't just make an exception and decide on his own to let Sofia Jo and Sadie into the park when the sign clearly stated 'NO DOGS ALLOWED IN THE PARK.'

Ava's grandfather listened carefully as the policeman explained his position. When the officer finished speaking, Pop-Pop nodded, understanding the situation, even if it wasn't the answer they had hoped for. "Thank you for your time," Ava's grandfather said kindly, offering a handshake. He appreciated that the policeman had taken the time to listen to their concerns, even if he couldn't help them directly.

As Ava and her grandfather began to walk back to their car, the policeman called out after them. "Good luck, Ava," he said warmly, giving her a reassuring smile. "I hope you can help your friend." He paused for a moment, his brow furrowed in thought, before adding, "You know, I agree with you both. It does seem unfair that Sofia Jo can't bring Sadie into the park. But unfortunately, I don't have the power to change the rules."

Just as Ava and her grandfather were about to leave, the policeman suddenly stopped them. "Wait a minute," he said, as a new idea seemed to come to him. "The mayor of our town is my boss. Maybe she could help you. She has more authority when it comes to changing things like this."

Ava's eyes lit up with a flicker of hope, and she glanced up at her grandfather, who nodded in agreement. "Thank you for the suggestion," he said, his voice filled with renewed determination. They both knew this was a small step forward, but it was something to hold on to. They thanked the policeman once again and then continued on their way, feeling a bit more hopeful as they left the park.

CHAPTER SEVEN

Back to Work

As they drove back to Ava's house, it was very quiet in the car. The excitement and hope that Ava felt on the ride to the park had vanished. She was crestfallen and disappointed. When they were almost home, Ava's grandfather looked at her and said, "Do you want to give up?"

"No," said Ava, although she had no idea of what to do next.

Determinedly, her grandfather responded, "Okay, then we won't give up!"

Ava glanced at her grandfather. He was once again smiling, which helped cause her disillusionment to somewhat fade and her hopes to climb.

When they finally arrived at Ava's home, the drive having given her much to think about, her grandfather turned to her with a gentle smile. "I think we should start fresh in the morning," he suggested, his voice full of encouragement. "I'll come by early so we can get right back to work on solving Sofia Jo's problem."

Ava nodded eagerly, feeling a renewed sense of determination. After a quick kiss on the cheek and a warm hug, she hopped out of the car and raced up to her front door. Her earlier worries seemed to fade away as she thought about the new plan they would tackle in the morning. Once again, Ava felt that familiar surge of excitement and hope bubbling up inside her.

As she slipped inside her house, Ava reflected on everything her grandfather had explained during their day together. The idea of the three branches of government was still a bit confusing, with so many different parts and roles to understand. But she didn't mind the challenge. She knew that helping Sofia Jo would take more than just good intentions—it would take hard work, careful thinking, and perhaps a little bit of patience too.

But most of all, Ava realized how lucky she was to have a grandfather like Pop-Pop, someone who always kept his promises and never gave up on her. That thought filled her with a comforting warmth as she drifted off to sleep that night. And just as he had said, bright and early the next morning, there was her grandfather, knocking on the door, ready to continue together.

It was the start of another beautiful summer day, and they decided to continue their work at the picnic table in Ava's back yard. "What? No lemonade?" her grandfather asked.

"Isn't it too early in the morning for lemonade, Pop-Pop?"

"Absolutely not!" he answered. "It isn't too early for cookies either," he said with a laugh. "I know this is definitely **not** brain food. However, 'everything in moderation' is the advice my grandfather gave me when I was your age," he said.

While laughing, Ava went back inside the house to get the lemonade and cookies. She had to admit this was yet another good idea from her grandfather. They were both still laughing as Ava placed the tray of lemonade and cookies on the picnic table between them. The duo was now ready to continue with their quest.

CHAPTER EIGHT

Pop-Pop's Cabin

Days passed, but Ava and Pop-Pop continued strategizing as to how best to help Sofia Jo. "Ava, before we start today, I think we could use a change of venue!" Pop-Pop proclaimed. "What's a change of venue?" asked Ava. "A change of venue under the law can happen for a variety of reasons, but for our purposes today, it simply means a change in our location. What if we take the hour ride up to my cabin on the lake to continue our work? We can pack and take some sandwiches and fruit with us, as long as we don't forget the lemonade and cookies," he laughingly suggested. Ava thought this to be a fantastic idea, especially for something with such a silly name as a change of venue.

Pop-Pop's cozy and very small cabin was one of Ava's very favorite places. The cabin was nestled at the feet of several caverns, backed by a low mountain range and set on the shore of a dark blue placid lake. The structure itself was surrounded by many colored wildflowers, which remained evident and vibrant under the light of the moon.

Ava's grandfather had painted a large American flag on one full side of the cabin's roof to celebrate the existence of the United States of America and to honor the sacrifice his son (Ava's father) had made during World War II.

On the ride to the cabin, Pop-Pop had another terrific idea which met with Ava's full approval. He suggested they taste several of the cookies they had packed. And so they did. While happily munching, Pop-Pop turned to Ava and asked where her favorite place to read was located. Ava exclaimed, "I have more than one favorite place, Pop-Pop!" "What do you mean?" he asked. "Well, I like to do my homework and school reading in my bedroom because it is quiet, my desk is right there, and so are most of my school supplies." "That makes sense," said her grandfather.

"Where do you choose to read books other than those connected to school assignments? For instance, what about mysteries, scary books, biographies, or others, which may have caught your attention for either fun or learning or even both?" "I like to read outside if the weather is nice and even on the porch when it is raining or not too cold," she answered. "What about you, Pop-Pop? Do you like to read in different places?" she curiously asked.

Ava's grandfather didn't immediately answer her. She guessed that he still had some cookies in his mouth but then noticed he wasn't chewing anymore. She then easily recognized the look on his face when he was thinking. "Do you remember when I first mentioned the subject of civics to you?" "Yes, I do," she admitted. "And do you remember telling me that you didn't know what civics was about?" "I do," she said. "If you remember, I then explained to you that sometimes solving problems and helping others may require you to learn and think about subjects, ideas, and questions in ways you have never thought about before. Correct?"

"Yes, Pop-Pop, I remember," said Ava.

"Sometimes, I find coming to my cabin helps me think and solve problems more easily than I can at other locations. I'm not totally sure why, but the important thing is that I recognize this in myself. I am telling you this because you may find the same experience one day. You must pay attention to your feelings and know yourself well, or you may never experience it."

"We are here!" Pop-Pop pronounced after a considerable silence. I suggest we take a short walk, smell the flowers, and listen to the lake before we resume fighting for Sofia Jo." Brushing the cookie crumbs from her face, Ava grinned and nodded.

CHAPTER NINE

The Letter

L et's re-start our thinking," Ava's grandfather said. "So far we have learned from the park policeman that the executive branch of our government may not be able to help us in the way we had hoped. However, I still think we should try what the policeman suggested and ask the mayor directly if she could help us, even though she is also part of the executive branch. What do you think?"

"I definitely think we should try," replied Ava. "I do as well," confirmed her grandfather.

With her grandfather's assistance, Ava wrote a letter to the mayor of her town. She explained how the law was keeping Sofia Jo out of the park because she needed her seeing-eye dog Sadie to keep her safe while she enjoyed the park like everyone else. She admitted to the mayor that the existing law may seem like a good law and may have been written for seemingly good reasons. But she also raised a very intriguing question. She asked that if, in fact, the law was good, then why was it so unfair to Sofia Jo.

Ava had never actually met the mayor face-to-face, but she did remember seeing her once at the grand opening of the park. It had been a big day, filled with excitement and celebration, and the mayor had stood out among the crowd. Ava recalled how the mayor had worn a beautiful green dress that flowed elegantly as she moved, catching the sunlight in a way that made the fabric shimmer. She also wore big, black-framed sunglasses that gave her a look of importance, but her smile was warm and welcoming.

What Ava remembered most vividly was the mayor's long red hair, which seemed to glow like fire under the bright sun. Her face had a kind expression, with a pleasant smile that reached her eyes, making her seem approachable and friendly. The mayor wasn't alone that day—her husband had been by her side, along with their three young children, who looked excited to be a part of the event. They all seemed like a happy, close-knit family, and the mayor had taken the time to greet everyone she met with genuine warmth.

Seeing how friendly the mayor had been with everyone gave Ava a spark of hope. She thought that maybe, just maybe, the mayor would be the one to help Sofia Jo. After all, someone who was so kind and approachable might understand why it was so important for Sofia Jo to be able to bring Sadie into the park. With this hopeful thought in mind, Ava felt a little less anxious about the next steps she and her grandfather would take.

When Ava's letter was finished, her grandfather drove her to the post office on their way home from the cabin, and they mailed the letter together. "What do we do now, Pop-Pop?" she asked as the letter disappeared into the big blue mailbox.

"We wait," said her grandfather. And wait, they did. It seemed like a long time to Ava. The waiting seemed like the hardest part. "Just have patience," her grandfather told her.

After checking her mailbox faithfully every day for two long weeks, a letter finally arrived that looked very different from the others. It was in a long, shiny white envelope with a large gold seal and an eagle stamped on it. It was from the mayor of Ava's town!

Ava immediately called her grandfather and excitedly told him the letter from the mayor had finally arrived. She asked Pop-Pop to come to her house as soon as he could so they could open the letter together.

That evening, as the skies darkened and the wind began to howl, Ava's grandfather arrived at her house in the midst of a fierce rainstorm. The rain came down in heavy sheets, drenching everything in its path, while loud claps of thunder echoed through the air, shaking the windows. Lightning bolts split the sky, their jagged lines lighting up the night like bright yellow and white spider webs stretching across the heavens. Ava watched the storm from the window, her heart pounding a little faster with each flash of lightning. She couldn't help but wonder if the storm was a bad omen, a sign that things might not go as they hoped.

Despite the storm, her grandfather made his way to the front door, water dripping from his coat and hat. Ava quickly let him in, grateful to see him safe and sound. As they stepped inside, the warmth of the house provided some comfort, but the storm outside still rumbled ominously, a reminder of the uncertainty they were facing.

Her grandfather sat down on the couch in the cozy living room, still dripping from the rain. Ava hurried to fetch him a hand towel and the letter that had been waiting so anxiously to be opened. She handed him the towel first, watching as he dried his wet hands, the tension in the room almost palpable. The usual lightheartedness of their time together, often filled with lemonade and cookies, was absent now. All thoughts of their usual treats were pushed aside, replaced by the pressing concern of what the mayor's letter would reveal.

Ava sat down beside her grandfather, her eyes fixed on the letter that seemed to hold all the answers they were waiting for. The sound of the rain pounding against the windows and the distant rumble of thunder only heightened the anticipation, as they both wondered what the mayor had to say and whether it would bring them closer to helping Sofia Jo.

Her grandfather read the mayor's letter aloud. The mayor was very polite and thanked Ava for her letter. However, she said that she could not help Sofia Jo. She went on to explain that even though she was the mayor of the town, she could not just change the law nor make a special exception on her own. The mayor said that it wouldn't be correct, or within her governmental power, to change the law by herself, even if she agreed with Ava about the law being unfair to Sofia Jo. The mayor concluded her letter by explaining since the town legislature wrote the law, only they could change it.

Ava was crushed and again felt disappointed and discouraged. Their idea had not worked. Once again, Ava felt she had failed in her effort to help her friend.

CHAPTER TEN

A Second Letter

As they sat together quietly listening to the storm, Ava looked forlornly at her grandfather. She couldn't believe it. Her grandfather looked at her with great compassion. "Are you ready to give up now, Ava?" he asked.

"What else can we do, Pop-Pop?" "Do you still think that the law is good but unfair?" he asked. "Yes," she answered. "I do."

He looked down at his hands and then at Ava's face. "Do you still think this idea about changing the law is worth fighting for?" he asked.

"Yes, very much so," she said.

"Then let's see if we can think of a next step," said her grandfather. "Early tomorrow morning, with lemonade and cookies?" he asked. Ava beamed in response. She then tightly hugged her grandfather with renewed hope.

The following morning, Ava and her grandfather headed for the cabin and once again went to work trying to solve Sofia Jo's problem. Ava's grandfather started the conversation. "We found that the executive branch could not help us. The mayor explained to us in her letter that she couldn't change the law by herself. She felt that one person shouldn't change a law that was written by many. The mayor understood that our system of government was formed with three branches and that each branch has its own duties. The role of the legislative branch is to write the law as well as changing those laws in any way. Ava, I think the mayor is correct. I believe our next step should be to contact the legislative branch. After all, they wrote the 'NO DOGS ALLOWED IN THE PARK' law."

Ava thought for a moment, looked at her grandfather, and asked, "Is a law good just because most people believe it to be good?"

Her grandfather looked at Ava proudly and exclaimed, "That is another very good question, Ava. Let me ask you this. Suppose you were exploring and playing in the woods with a group of your friends, and your entire group got lost, and everyone was trying to decide which path to take to get everyone home safely. Most of your friends decided to choose the path with the most trees. Only a few of your friends decided to take the path with the most flowers. Just because the larger group chose the path with the most trees, it didn't necessarily mean that was the right path, did it?" he asked.

"No," Ava answered.

"Correct," said her grandfather. "It's the same concept when it comes to laws and rules. Just because a majority of the people decide that a certain law is good or right doesn't always make it so."

"This is especially true if a law negatively affects the basic rights of citizens in determining how they are treated," he continued. "Let me give you an example.

Not so long ago in our country, most people agreed with laws that allowed people to own black persons as slaves. Do you think those laws were good just because more people than not said so?" he asked.

"Of course not," said Ava. "But what does this have to do with helping Sofia Jo?" "You'll see. Have patience, Ava," instructed her grandfather. Ava slowly let out a long, exasperated breath.

"We have been doing a lot of intense thinking," said her grandfather, "and I think it is time for another letter. This time, as I mentioned earlier, we will send your letter directly to the legislature since they themselves wrote the 'NO DOGS ALLOWED IN THE PARK' law."

"What should I say in the letter to the legislature?" Ava asked.

"You will explain to them how the law may have been written for good reasons, but it is unfair to Sofia Jo by denying her entry to the park because she cannot bring her seeing-eye dog Sadie with her. You'll also ask the legislature to change the law," he said.

"Do you think it will work?" Ava hopefully asked. "I don't know. You can only try," her grandfather answered.

That is exactly what Ava did. Pop-Pop again helped her compose the letter, which was very similar to the letter Ava had previously sent to the mayor. When the letter was complete, Ava's grandfather drove her to the post office once again, and she mailed the letter.

Ava and her grandfather again had to wait for an answer to Ava's letter. This time, the wait was longer than before. Although Ava was becoming impatient, her grandfather explained that the reason for the longer wait was because all of the people in the legislature had to discuss Ava's request. Ava's first letter to the mayor only had to be answered by the mayor herself.

Ava listened, trying to understand why it had to be this way, but patience wasn't easy when something so important was at stake. Days turned into weeks, and the waiting seemed endless. Ava's thoughts often drifted to Sofia Jo and Sadie, imagining how much happier they would be if the law was changed.

Then, finally, after what felt like an eternity, a letter arrived at Ava's home. As soon as she saw the envelope, her heart skipped a beat. It bore the same gold seal and eagle emblem as the letter from the mayor, and Ava knew instantly that this was the response they had been waiting for. The sight of that seal made her even more anxious than before, her hands trembling slightly as she held the envelope. She could hardly contain her excitement and nerves, and she found herself glancing out the window repeatedly, hoping to catch a glimpse of her grandfather's car pulling up.

When her grandfather finally arrived, Ava practically flew to the door to greet him. Together, they sat down, the unopened letter resting between them. Ava's mind raced with possibilities. Despite her nervousness, she felt a strong sense of confidence in her request. She believed deep down that the lawmakers in the legislature would see the fairness in what she was asking and would agree to change the law.

As they prepared to open the letter, Ava couldn't help but picture the moment she would rush to Sofia Jo with the good news, her heart swelling with the thought of seeing her friend's face light up with happiness. This was the moment they had been waiting for, and Ava's hope and determination had never been stronger.

As soon as her grandfather arrived, they immediately ripped opened the envelope. The men and women in the legislature were very nice and extremely polite in their answers. But they still denied Ava's request to change the law. Ava was very surprised and more disappointed than when the mayor turned down her request. Mostly, she felt miserable for her friend Sofia Jo. It just didn't seem fair. Ava felt that she had failed her friend yet again. She looked up at her grandfather and was met with his seemingly never-ending and supportive smile.

"Ava, my dear granddaughter, are you ready to give up yet?" he asked. "Not a chance," she said determinedly. "What's next?"

Chapter Eleven

Never Give Up

"**D**o you still think this law, which you have agreed was written for good reasons, is bad?" her grandfather asked one more time.

"Absolutely," Ava answered.

"Then let's see if we can think of another approach to help your friend." Ava felt extremely lucky to have a grandfather who didn't want to give up either.

"Ava, do you remember our earlier civics lesson, including the number of branches included in our government?" her grandfather asked.

"Yes, there are three branches, Pop-Pop. They are called the executive, legislative, and judicial branches," she answered.

"Correct. So, are you ready to power-up your brain again?" "I am *very* ready," she laughingly answered.

"Alright, but first, I think we need more brain food," he said with a wink and a laugh. By this time, Ava knew the drill and was back in a flash with their packed lunches, fruit, lemonade, and, of course, more cookies for their excursion to the cabin.

After enjoying their lunch, Ava's grandfather put down his glass and began. "Remember, the purpose of the legislative branch is to write the laws. The purpose of the executive branch is to enforce the laws written by the legislative branch. The purpose of the third branch of our government, the judicial branch, is to explain and interpret the laws and also to make sure that the laws do not treat people unequally by treating people differently from each other for no good or valid reason. As you can see, each branch of our government has its own purposes and powers, which are separate from each other. This is called the separation of powers," he explained.

"Why are the three powers kept separate?" asked Ava.

"For a very simple but important reason," said her grandfather. "The three different branches of government are kept separate to prevent any one person or institution from becoming too powerful. If one person, for example, a king, not only wrote the laws but also enforced and interpreted them, there could easily be an abuse of power, which could harm everyone. For instance, if we were ruled by a king who wrote a law, and you believed the law to be bad because it treated people unfairly, who would you turn to for fairness and justice?"

"I don't know," she answered.

"We would have only the king to rely upon, the same king who wrote the law! Is the king going to interpret the very law he wrote and decide he wrote a bad law which was unfair? That would be highly unlikely.

Someone who may have been treated unfairly by the law would have been stuck," he explained.

"Like Sofia Jo?" Ava asked.

"Exactly," said her grandfather. "That's why our system of government is designed to protect all of us against such a possibility by separating the three powers among the three different branches of government. Do you understand?" he asked.

"I think so," answered Ava.

"As you are well aware, we have tried to help Sofia Jo by attempting to utilize the legislative and executive branches of our government," he said. "How do you think we have done so far?"

Ava looked sideways at her grandfather, "Not good, Pop-Pop." Her grandfather laughed long, loud, and hard at Ava's answer. His laughter was so infectious it even forced Ava to smile.

"We are now left with the third branch of our government, which is the judicial branch," said her grandfather.

Ava then again asked, "What's our next step?"

"We will ask our judge, who works in the courthouse and who is part of the judicial branch, to declare this otherwise good law to be a bad law. Again, we're not taking this step because the reasons for the law are bad, but rather, because those good reasons are not good enough to justifiably and fairly prevent Sofia Jo and others requiring service dogs from entering the park," he answered.

Ava was exuberant that there was still another opportunity to help Sofia Jo. "But what about the good reasons for the law, Pop-Pop? What will the judge say about that?" she asked. Her grandfather said they needed to think of a way to convince the judge that the good reasons for the law were not important enough to deny her disabled friend's access to the park. In addition, the good reasons for the law could still be largely accomplished and not lost by allowing Sofia Jo and her dog Sadie admission to the park.

"Do you remember the good reasons the legislature had for writing the law not allowing dogs into the park?" he asked Ava.

"Some of them," she answered.

"Let's discuss them to determine if our planned arguments to the court are reasonable and will hold water," he said. "I am all ears," said Ava.

"One good reason for the law disallowing dogs in the park is because they may use the park grounds as their bathroom, which may create an unclean condition. This could be remedied by requiring those accompanied by service dogs to immediately clean up after them."

"Another good reason for the law disallowing dogs in the park is because some dogs are not friendly, or are nervous or afraid, and could bite someone. But service dogs are trained to be friendly and not bite. They are also given special identification to wear so that people would be aware of who they are," he continued.

"Ava, do you remember any of the other good reasons for the law?" asked her grandfather.

"Yes, I do. Small dogs could accidentally trip someone, and large dogs could accidentally knock someone over. What can we say to the judge about that, Pop-Pop?" Her grandfather replied they could explain to the judge that seeing-eye dogs are highly trained service dogs, having been taught to be very careful around young children and older adults, like grandfathers and grandmothers.

"Can you remember any of the other good reasons for not allowing dogs in the park?" he prodded.

Ava thought a moment and responded. "Yes, another good reason for not allowing dogs in the park is that some dogs don't get along with other dogs or other animals, which could lead to them fighting with each other, which could be dangerous. What could we say to the judge about that, Pop-Pop?"

Her grandfather said they could inform the judge that a service dog's training teaches them not to fight with other dogs and to ignore other animals while assisting their owner. "In addition, we could remind the judge that we are not saying that the entire law is bad. We are not asking that the law be changed to allow all dogs in the park, only seeing-eye and other service dogs, which are needed to protect their owners. There would be no dog fighting if the only dogs allowed were trained service dogs," he added.

"Are there any other good reasons we discussed for not allowing dogs in the park that you can remember?" Ava's grandfather asked. She tried to remember but couldn't recall any others. "What about the fact that some children and adults are simply afraid of dogs? Do you think it would be fair to allow dogs in the park when some people wouldn't visit because of their fear of dogs?" he asked Ava.

"No, I don't," said Ava, who sounded a little worried about the effect of her answer.

But seeing the worry on Ava's face, her grandfather quickly stepped in to reassure her. He knew how much this meant to her and how important it was to find the right words to convince the judge. "Ava," he began gently, placing a comforting hand on her shoulder, "we can explain to the judge that service dogs, like Sadie, are different from other dogs. They're equipped with special leashes and harnesses that clearly identify them as service animals. These special tools let everyone know that these dogs have an important job to do."

Ava listened closely, her heart lifting a little with each word. Her grandfather continued, his voice calm and full of the wisdom she always admired. "And it's not just about the equipment they wear," he added. "Service dogs are specially trained to stay by their owners' sides at all times. They're taught not to get distracted, not to wander off, and most importantly, to keep their owners safe. Because of this training, there's really no reason for anyone to be afraid of these dogs. They're not just pets—they're protectors and helpers, like Sadie is for Sofia Jo."

Ava nodded, feeling a wave of relief wash over her. Her grandfather's explanation made so much sense, and it gave her a renewed sense of hope. She imagined standing in front of the judge, explaining how Sadie's presence wasn't just necessary but also completely safe for everyone around her. Ava knew that with her grandfather's guidance, they would be able to show the judge that Sofia Jo and Sadie deserved to be together in the park, just like everyone else.

CHAPTER TWELVE

The 14ᵗʰ Amendment to the United States Constitution

Ava's summer was rapidly transforming her school vacation into a life-long educational journey of a type she had never previously experienced. This was made possible and created by the teachings of her grandfather coupled with Ava's deep desire to help her friend. She felt proud of herself while recognizing the extent and importance of her contribution to their joint endeavor of assisting Sofia Jo.

Ava was pleasantly surprised when her grandfather telephoned her in the middle of the week following their previous weekend's work session.

"Can we meet this afternoon and get some ice cream?" he asked.

"What time?" Ava asked. "I will pick you up in fifteen minutes."

"Great! I will see you soon," she exclaimed.

As they enjoyed their three-scoop cones on the outside deck of their favorite ice cream shop, Ava noticed Pop-Pop obviously had something on his mind. "You have learned so much and worked so hard. I think it is time to pause our work, summarize our efforts thus far, and carefully plan our next steps," her grandfather explained. "Doing so will help me to organize my thoughts. What do you think, Ava?"

"I agree. I think it will help me as well," she said.

"I'm glad you agree. Let me start this way. I'm sure you recall that our Constitution established our form of government, including its three branches, each having its own separate duties and powers. You have also learned that the unique powers of the executive, legislative, and judicial branches were specifically given to each separately by our Founding Fathers in order to prevent an abuse of power by balancing those powers among them. I now read to you aloud that part of the 14th Amendment to our Constitution, which I feel speaks directly to Sofia Jo's situation."

> *All persons born or naturalized in the United States... are citizens of the United States and of the State wherein they reside.*

> *No State shall make or enforce any law which shall abridge the privileges or immunities of citizens of the United States... nor deny to any person within its jurisdiction the equal protection of the laws...*

"Ava, do you remember agreeing to the concept that just because more people than not vote a certain way or make a choice by their majority vote doesn't necessarily make their choice right?" her grandfather asked.

"Yes, I do," answered Ava. "I remember the examples of incorrect choices made by those who chose a certain path out of the woods, as well as those who chose a right of slavery over other human beings."

"Good. I hope my reading of the 14th Amendment gives you a better understanding of how our Constitution is written to protect all of us, even those who may not be in the majority. This is one of the main reasons we have the 14th Amendment, also known as the Equal Protection Clause, as part of our Constitution. The 14th Amendment provides the judicial branch the opportunity, power, and duty to override a majority vote when the will of the people results in a law which wrongfully discriminates against a segment or part of our society."

Pop-Pop continued. "It is very important to understand that our judges, as part of the judicial branch, have the last word in determining the constitutionality of our laws written by the legislative branch. In other words, the U.S. Constitution, as interpreted by our courts, serves as the supreme law of our land."

CHAPTER THIRTEEN

The Judge and Decision of the Court

Ava's grandfather finished his ice cream, took a deep and satisfying breath, looked at Ava, and said, "My dear granddaughter, I think it's time to put into action our final idea to help Sofia Jo."

"How do we use what you've taught me about our Constitution to help Sofia Jo?" Ava asked.

"As Sofia Jo's lawyer, and with you as my assistant, we will ask the judge to rule that the law not allowing dogs in the park shouldn't apply to seeing-eye and other service dogs. We explain to the judge that we agree the law may have been written for good reasons. Sometimes, however, seemingly good reasons aren't enough to keep a good law from being bad," he concluded.

"As you have come to learn, our Constitution is meant to guard and protect us against all laws, good or bad, well-intentioned or otherwise, which have the effect of treating people unfairly or unequally and thereby denying each of us equal protection under the law. That is what the 'NO DOGS ALLOWED IN THE PARK' law does. The law, as it stands, with no changes, has the effect of discriminating against Sofia Jo by denying her entry to the park because her disability requires her service-dog Sadie to be by her side. All the good reasons for the law are not important enough to exclude Sofia Jo and Sadie from entering and enjoying the park," he continued. "We will argue to the judge that the good reasons for the law can still be largely satisfied without treating Sofia Jo differently from others because of her blindness. Because of this, we will ask the judge to rule that the 'NO DOGS ALLOWED IN THE PARK' law may have been enacted with good intentions and even for good reasons, but it is in violation of our Constitution's requirement prohibiting the denial to any person the equal protection of our laws," he explained.

That's exactly what Ava's grandfather did. He wrote and filed their request with the court.

"Pop-Pop, now what do we do?" asked Ava. "We wait," he answered. "*Again!*" proclaimed a frustrated Ava.

"Again," her grandfather affirmed, chuckling at his granddaughter's good-natured exasperation.

Months passed. Finally, one day after school, Ava's grandfather called her and said the court had scheduled a date the following week to hear their arguments against the law. Ava felt fearful and anxious but had faith in her grandfather and in her belief that the law was unfair.

When the day of the court hearing arrived, Ava's grandfather, along with Ava, Ava's mother, Sofia Jo, and Sofia Jo's parents, drove to the courthouse together in Pop-Pop's station wagon. Everyone was very quiet and still, except for Sadie, who seemed happy just to be with everyone going for a ride. After parking the car, they all walked together up the multiple steps to the courthouse. Ava silently wondered if everyone felt as apprehensive as she did.

When Ava, her mother, her grandfather, Sofia Jo and Sofia Jo's parents arrived at the courthouse, the air was filled with a sense of anticipation. As they approached the entrance, the courthouse security officer, standing tall in his uniform, noticed Sadie by their side and immediately stepped forward to stop them. Ava felt a moment of panic, worrying that this might be another barrier they would have to overcome. But her grandfather remained calm and pointed to the special vest that Sadie was wearing—a vest that clearly identified her as a service dog. The officer inspected the vest carefully, noting the official markings that showed Sadie's important role. With a nod of understanding, he stepped aside and ushered them all inside, including Sadie.

Once inside the courthouse, they quickly realized that the usual bustling crowd was nowhere to be seen. The hallway leading to the courtroom was quiet, and when they entered the courtroom itself, they found it almost completely empty. The absence of other cases gave the room a still, solemn atmosphere, as if the day had been set aside just for them. Ava's heart beat faster as she took in the quiet space, realizing how significant this moment was.

They soon learned that their case was the only one being heard by the judge that day, which explained the emptiness of the courtroom. The attorneys for the town's legislature had filed a written opposition to Sofia Jo's request—an official document for the judge to review—but they had chosen not to appear in person. This decision puzzled Ava's grandfather, who had expected a more formal opposition. It seemed that the attorneys believed their reasons for writing the law were strong enough to stand on their own, and that the town's authority was clear and justified.

Even though the absence of the opposing attorneys was unexpected, Ava's grandfather remained focused. He guided Ava, her mother, Sofia Jo, Sofia Jo's parents and Sadie to the front row of seats, where they settled in with a mix of nerves and determination. Then, with a calm confidence, he continued down the aisle to the area where the lawyers were required to sit—right in front of the judge's bench. As he walked, Ava couldn't help but feel a deep sense of pride in her grandfather. This was the moment they had worked so hard for, and she knew he would do everything he could to make sure their voices were heard.

Ava curiously looked at her surroundings and was impressed with, as well as a little intimidated by, the enormous size of the courtroom and the dark, gleaming wood throughout the space. The large wall clock could be heard ticking down the seconds as they waited in silence for the judge to appear.

Her grandfather swiveled around in his chair, winked, and smiled at his small gallery. They nervously smiled back at him. Ava, ever so proud, didn't realize that her mind's eye had just snapped a picture of her grandfather. The memory of that moment would return to her many years later when, as a young lawyer, Ava would tenderly brush a light dusting of snow from his grave marker. It was a special, life-long gift of an unforgettable memory of her precious grandfather.

Just as she was picking a loose thread from her dress, Ava heard a heavy door open and a loud, stern voice exclaim, "Please rise, Judge Segal presiding." Everyone in the courtroom stood as the judge entered from a door behind the bench and took his seat.

"Please be seated," the judge said as he peered down from his perch on the bench. The group sat down in unison. Judge Segal's dark eyes briefly examined each of them. Ava even thought she saw a very slight smile on the judge's face when he noticed Sadie sitting quietly next to them. However, she remembered her grandfather's words of warning when she had expressed to him her hope that the judge 'liked dogs.' In a serious tone of voice, Pop-Pop explained to her that the judge's like or dislike of dogs would have no impact on his decision, nor should it. A judge must put aside his or her personal views in deciding whether a law treats people unequally without sufficient reason.

After silently reviewing and re-reading the application and supporting documents on his desk, the judge looked at Ava's grandfather and said, "I will hear your argument now, counselor."

Ava's grandfather immediately stood up, introduced himself, wished the judge a good morning, and began to address Sofia Jo's request. He explained why they were there and what he was requesting of the court regarding the 'NO DOGS ALLOWED IN THE PARK' law.

As the hearing progressed, Ava was surprised to hear the judge challenge her grandfather regarding the good reasons for the law. Her grandfather's answers, however, were no surprise. She remembered how they had previously discussed those good reasons in preparation for today and now understood why that preparation was necessary.

Her grandfather respectfully explained to the judge that he agreed the law was written for good reasons and with good intentions. But Pop- Pop also argued that the good reasons behind the law still didn't justify excluding Sofia Jo from the park.

Finally, he argued that the law was in violation of our Constitution, which granted to everyone equal protection under our laws. This particular law treated Sofia Jo unequally and unfairly by denying her entrance to the park as a result of her needs created solely due to her disability. For that reason, the law should be struck down.

When Ava's grandfather was finished, he respectfully thanked the judge and returned to his seat to await the ruling of the court.

The judge was very quiet for a long time while he thought about Sofia Jo's arguments against the law.

Finally, the judge raised his head and began to speak. Ava noticed that he again looked at each one of them, as well as her grandfather. "Today, you have asked this court to do something very significant and of great import," he stated. "You have asked this court to declare a law written for good reasons by our Legislature to be invalid. You must understand that under our form of government, with its separation of powers, it is the function of the legislative branch to write the laws, *not* the judicial branch!"

Ava looked down at her feet and felt a little sick to her stomach as she grasped the judge's admonishment. She looked at Sofia Jo and her parents; without uttering a word, the group expressed a collective sense of uncertainty.

The judge continued. "Although it is not the function of this court to write our laws, it is the function, as well as the duty, of the judicial branch to ensure our laws comply with the supreme law of our land, which is the United States Constitution. This duty remains, regardless of whether or not a law is agreed upon by many or by few. Our Constitution demands that everyone be treated equally under the law."

"That being said, it is the ruling of this court that the law which reads and enforces 'NO DOGS ALLOWED IN THE PARK' is invalid. Even though the law was written for good reasons, it results in the unfair discrimination and exclusion of those whose disabilities require the use of service dogs to access and enjoy the town's public recreational spaces. For that reason, this court declares the law in its present form to be unconstitutional as being in violation of the Equal Protection Clause of the U.S. Constitution and, therefore, unenforceable."

CHAPTER FOURTEEN

The Significance of Success

A va couldn't believe it. They won! She was also well aware of the fact that this victory went beyond just helping Sofia Jo. It was a victory for all disabled persons who rely on service dogs, as well as an affirmation for our form of government. It was a wonderful ride home from the courthouse for so many reasons. Ava couldn't remember a happier day in her life. It was a delightful mixture of happiness, pride, and relief.

Shortly after learning of the judge's ruling, the town legislature formally amended the law to read 'NO DOGS ALLOWED IN THE PARK, EXCEPT SEEING EYE DOGS AND OTHER SERVICE DOGS.'

The mayor and the park policeman were pleased with the amendment. The happiest people, however, of course, were Ava, Ava's mother, Sofia Jo and her family, and Ava's grandfather, Zachary Joseph. It just so happened the judge's ruling also resulted in Sadie being an even happier dog than she was before. Over the next several months, Sadie would make many new service canine friends while accompanying Sofia Jo to the park.

Ava could hardly believe what they had accomplished together. The realization of their success filled her with a deep sense of pride and amazement. Without hesitation, she threw her arms around her grandfather in a tight hug, her heart overflowing with gratitude. "Thank you, Pop-Pop," she whispered, her voice full of emotion. She knew that without his guidance and support, they might never have reached this moment.

Her grandfather returned the hug with a warm smile, his eyes shining with pride. "Ava," he said softly, "I'm so very proud of you. You never gave up, even when things were tough and it required so much hard work, thought, and patience. You've shown remarkable strength and determination." Though he didn't say it out loud, Pop-Pop was deeply inspired by what he had witnessed. He had seen his granddaughter's innocent idealism transform into a fierce resolve to make things right. It was a change that touched him beyond words, a testament to Ava's growing understanding of the world and her place in it.

That summer, Ava learned so much—not just about the government and the importance of laws, but about herself. She discovered how powerful one could become when determination was combined with learning and knowledge. This newfound understanding made her feel proud of her country, a place where the Constitution and a republican form of government existed to protect its citizens. She felt thankful for living in a land where these principles could be used to stand up for what was right.

As Ava reflected on everything she had learned, she also thought more about her father's sacrifice. Though she had been too young to remember him, she often held his Purple Heart medal, studying it with a mix of curiosity and reverence. The medal represented honor and bravery, but for Ava, it also symbolized the deep loss she felt—the absence of a father she never got to know. The medal, while inspiring, seemed like a small consolation for the void left in her life. Yet, through this experience, Ava began to appreciate the true meaning of her father's sacrifice more deeply. She understood that his actions, like those of many others, were part of the reason she could live in a country where justice and freedom were valued so highly.

In the end, Ava realized that this journey had not only been about helping Sofia Jo but also about discovering her own strength and the powerful legacy her father had left behind.

Ava had also come to a full realization and understanding of the important lesson somehow communicated to her in that mysterious dream which she had experienced so many months ago: one's fate, as well as the fate of others, can sometimes be influenced by the motives and actions of persons determined to make our world a better place.

The following week, Ava, Sofia Jo, and Sadie proudly and jointly entered the park for the first time. The policeman smiled and waved to them while pointing to a new sign, which included the amended law allowing entrance by all service dogs. What really made Ava's smile even larger that day, however, was the sight she saw next. Just inside the park's entrance, standing next to the three tall, bright green water fountains and three smaller ones, was a matching bright green low- to-the-ground water fountain, which was installed especially for Sadie so that she and all the other service animals could enjoy their well- deserved drinks*!*

The End

Author's Note: On July 26, 1990, President George H.W. Bush signed into Federal law, the "Americans with Disabilities Act" (ADA). One of the main purposes of the landmark legislation was to ensure persons with disabilities had full public access to their communities.

On September 25, 2008, President George W. Bush signed the "ADA Amendments Act of 2008" (ADAAA) into law. The amendment broadened the definition of 'disability,' thereby extending the ADA's protections to a greater number of people. The ADAAA also expanded the original ADA examples of 'major life activities' including, but not limited to, "caring for oneself, performing manual tasks seeing, hearing, eating, sleeping, walking, standing, lifting, bending, speaking, breathing, learning, reading, concentrating, thinking, communicating, and working." The U.S. House Committee on Education and Labor stated the amendment "makes it absolutely clear that the ADA is intended to provide broad coverage to protect anyone who faces discrimination on the basis of disability."

Declaration of Independence

DECLARATION OF INDEPENDENCE

IN CONGRESS, JULY 4, 1776

The Unanimous Declaration of the Thirteen United States of America

When in the Course of human events, it becomes necessary for one people to dissolve the political bands which have connected them with another and to assume among the powers of the earth, the separate and equal station to which the Laws of Nature and of Nature's God entitle them, a decent respect to the opinions of mankind requires that they should declare the causes which impel them to the separation.

We hold these truths to be self-evident: that all men are created equal, that they are endowed by their Creator with certain unalienable Rights, that among these are Life, Liberty, and the pursuit of Happiness. — That to secure these rights, Governments are instituted among Men, deriving their just powers from the consent of the governed — That whenever any Form of Government becomes destructive of these ends, it is the Right of the People to alter or to abolish it, and to institute new Government, laying its foundation on such principles and organizing its powers in such form, as to them shall seem most likely to effect their Safety and Happiness. Prudence, indeed, will dictate that Governments long established should not be changed for light and transient causes; and accordingly, all experience hath shewn that mankind are more disposed to suffer, while evils are sufferable than to right themselves by abolishing the forms to which they are accustomed. But when a long train of abuses and usurpations, pursuing invariably the same Object, evinces a design to reduce them under absolute Despotism, it is their right, it is their duty, to throw off such Government and to provide new Guards for their future security. — Such has been the patient sufferance of these Colonies; and such is now the necessity which constrains them to alter their former Systems of Government. The history of the present King of Great Britain is a history of repeated injuries and usurpations, all having in direct object the establishment of an absolute Tyranny over these States. To prove this, let Facts be submitted to a candid world.

He has refused his Assent to Laws, the most wholesome and necessary for the public good.

He has forbidden his Governors to pass Laws of immediate and pressing importance unless suspended in their operation till his Assent should be obtained, and when so suspended, he has utterly neglected to attend to them.

He has refused to pass other Laws for the accommodation of large districts of people unless those people would relinquish the right of Representation in the Legislature, a right inestimable to them and formidable to tyrants only.

He has called together legislative bodies at places unusual, uncomfortable, and distant from the depository of their Public Records for the sole purpose of fatiguing them into compliance with his measures.

He has dissolved Representative Houses repeatedly, for opposing with manly firmness his invasions on the rights of the people.

He has refused for a long time, after such dissolutions, to cause others to be elected, whereby the Legislative Powers, incapable of Annihilation, have returned to the People at large for their exercise; the State remaining in the mean time exposed to all the dangers of invasion from without, and convulsions within.

He has endeavoured to prevent the population of these States; for that purpose obstructing the Laws for Naturalization of Foreigners; refusing to pass others to encourage their migrations hither, and raising the conditions of new Appropriations of Lands.

He has obstructed the Administration of Justice by refusing his Assent to Laws for establishing Judiciary Powers.

He has made Judges dependent on his Will alone for the tenure of their offices and the amount and payment of their salaries.

He has erected a multitude of New Offices and sent hither swarms of Officers to harass our people and eat out their substance.

He has kept among us, in times of peace, Standing Armies without the Consent of our legislatures.

He has affected to render the Military independent of and superior to the Civil Power.

He has combined with others to subject us to a jurisdiction foreign to our constitution and unacknowledged by our laws, giving his Assent to their Acts of pretended Legislation:

For Quartering large bodies of armed troops among us:

For protecting them, by a mock Trial from punishment for any Murders which they should commit on the Inhabitants of these States:

For cutting off our Trade with all parts of the world: For imposing Taxes on us without our Consent:

For depriving us in many cases, of the benefit of Trial by Jury: For transporting us beyond Seas to be tried for pretended offences:

For abolishing the free System of English Laws in a neighbouring Province, establishing therein an Arbitrary government, and enlarging its Boundaries so as to render it at once an example and fit instrument for introducing the same absolute rule into these Colonies:

For taking away our Charters, abolishing our most valuable Laws and altering fundamentally the Forms of our Governments:

For suspending our own Legislatures, and declaring themselves invested with power to legislate for us in all cases whatsoever.

He has abdicated Government here, by declaring us out of his Protection and waging War against us.

He has plundered our seas, ravaged our coasts, burnt our towns, and destroyed the lives of our people.

He is at this time transporting large Armies of foreign Mercenaries to complete the works of death, desolation and tyranny, already begun with circumstances of Cruelty & perfidy scarcely paralleled in the most barbarous ages, and totally unworthy the Head of a civilized nation.

He has constrained our fellow Citizens taken Captive on the high Seas to bear Arms against their Country, to become the executioners of their friends and Brethren, or to fall themselves by their Hands.

He has excited domestic insurrections amongst us, and has endeavoured to bring on the inhabitants of our frontiers, the merciless Indian Savages whose known rule of warfare, is an undistinguished destruction of all ages, sexes and conditions.

In every stage of these Oppressions We have Petitioned for Redress in the most humble terms:

Our repeated Petitions have been answered only by repeated injury. A Prince whose character is thus marked by every act which may define a Tyrant, is unfit to be the ruler of a free people.

Nor have We been wanting in attentions to our British brethren. We have warned them from time to time of attempts by their legislature to extend an unwarrantable jurisdiction over us. We have reminded them of the circumstances of our emigration and settlement here. We have appealed to their native justice and magnanimity, and we have conjured them by the ties of our common kindred to disavow these usurpations, which, would inevitably interrupt our connections and correspondence. They too have been deaf to the voice of justice and of consanguinity. We must, therefore, acquiesce in the necessity, which denounces our Separation, and hold them, as we hold the rest of mankind, Enemies in War, in Peace Friends.

We, therefore, the Representatives of the united States of America, in General Congress, Assembled, appealing to the Supreme Judge of the world for the rectitude of our intentions, do, in the Name, and by Authority of the good People of these Colonies, solemnly publish and declare, That these United Colonies are, and of Right ought to be Free and Independent States; that they are Absolved from all Allegiance to the British Crown, and that all political connection between them and the State of Great Britain, is and ought to be totally dissolved; and that as Free and Independent States, they have full Power to levy War, conclude Peace, contract Alliances, establish Commerce, and to do all other Acts and Things which Independent States may of right do. And for the support of this Declaration, with a firm reliance on the protection of divine Providence, we mutually pledge to each other our Lives, our Fortunes and our sacred Honor.

[*The 56 signatures on the Declaration were arranged in six columns:*]

Georgia:

Button Gwinnett, Lyman Hall, George Walton

North Carolina:

William Hooper, Joseph Hewes, John Penn

South Carolina:

Edward Rutledge, Thomas Heyward, Jr., Thomas Lynch, Jr., Arthur Middleton

Maryland:

Samuel Chase, William Paca, Thomas Stone, Charles Carroll of Carrollton

Virginia:

George Wythe, Richard Henry Lee, Thomas Jefferson, Benjamin Harrison, Thomas Nelson, Jr., Francis Lightfoot Lee, Carter Braxton

Pennsylvania:

Robert Morris, Benjamin Rush, Benjamin Franklin, John Morton, George Clymer, James Smith, George Taylor, James Wilson, George Ross

Delaware:

Caesar Rodney, George Read, Thomas McKean

New York:

William Floyd, Philip Livingston, Francis Lewis, Lewis Morris

New Jersey:

Richard Stockton, John Witherspoon, Francis Hopkinson, John Hart, Abraham Clark

New Hampshire:

Josiah Bartlett, William Whipple, Matthew Thornton

Massachusetts:

John Hancock, Samuel Adams, John Adams, Robert Treat Paine, Elbridge Gerry

Rhode Island:

Stephen Hopkins, William Ellery

Connecticut:

Roger Sherman, Samuel Huntington, William Williams, Oliver Wolcott

The Constitution of the United States of America

THE CONSTITUTION OF THE UNITED STATES OF AMERICA

We the People of the United States, in Order to form a more perfect Union, establish Justice, insure domestic Tranquility, provide for the common defense, promote the general Welfare, and secure the Blessings of Liberty to ourselves and our Posterity, do ordain and establish this Constitution for the United States of America.

Article I

Section 1. All legislative Powers herein granted shall be vested in a Congress of the United States, which shall consist of a Senate and House of Representatives.

Section 2. The House of Representatives shall be composed of Members chosen every second Year by the People of the several States, and the Electors in each State shall have the Qualifications requisite for Electors of the most numerous Branch of the State Legislature.

No Person shall be a Representative who shall not have attained to the Age of twenty five Years, and been seven Years a Citizen of the United States, and who shall not, when elected, be an Inhabitant of that State in which he shall be chosen.

Representatives and direct Taxes shall be apportioned among the several States which may be included within this Union, according to their respective Numbers, which shall be determined by adding to the whole Number of free Persons, including those bound to Service for a Term of Years, and excluding Indians not taxed, three fifths of all other Persons. The actual Enumeration shall be made within three Years after the first Meeting of the Congress of the United States, and within every subsequent Term of ten Years, in such Manner as they shall by Law direct. The Number of Representatives shall not exceed one for every thirty Thousand, but each State shall have at Least one Representative; and until such enumeration shall be made, the State of New Hampshire shall be entitled to choose three, Massachusetts eight, Rhode- Island and Providence Plantations one, Connecticut five, New-York six, New Jersey four, Pennsylvania eight, Delaware one, Maryland six, Virginia ten, North Carolina five, South Carolina five, and Georgia three.

When vacancies happen in the Representation from any State, the Executive Authority thereof shall issue Writs of Election to fill such Vacancies.

The House of Representatives shall choose their Speaker and other Officers; and shall have the sole Power of Impeachment.

Section 3. The Senate of the United States shall be composed of two Senators from each State, chosen by the Legislature thereof, for six Years; and each Senator shall have one Vote.

Immediately after they shall be assembled in Consequence of the first Election, they shall be divided as equally as may be into three Classes. The Seats of the Senators of the first Class shall be vacated at the Expiration of the second Year, of the second Class at the Expiration of the fourth Year, and of the third Class at the Expiration of the sixth Year, so that one third may be chosen every second Year; and if Vacancies happen by Resignation, or otherwise, during the Recess of the Legislature of any State, the Executive thereof may make temporary Appointments until the next Meeting of the Legislature, which shall then fill such Vacancies.

No Person shall be a Senator who shall not have attained to the Age of thirty Years, and been nine Years a Citizen of the United States, and who shall not, when elected, be an Inhabitant of that State for which he shall be chosen.

The Vice President of the United States shall be President of the Senate, but shall have no Vote, unless they be equally divided.

The Senate shall choose their other Officers, and also a President pro tempore, in the Absence of the Vice President, or when he shall exercise the Office of President of the United States.

The Senate shall have the sole Power to try all Impeachments. When sitting for that Purpose, they shall be on Oath or Affirmation. When the President of the United States is tried, the Chief Justice shall preside: And no Person shall be convicted without the Concurrence of two thirds of the Members present.

Judgment in Cases of impeachment shall not extend further than to removal from office, and disqualification to hold and enjoy any Office of honor, Trust or Profit under the United States: but the Party convicted shall nevertheless be liable and subject to Indictment, Trial, Judgment, and Punishment, according to Law.

Section 4. The Times, Places, and Manner of holding Elections for Senators and Representatives shall be prescribed in each State by the Legislature thereof, but the Congress may at any time by Law make or alter such Regulations, except as to the Places of choosing Senators.

The Congress shall assemble at least once every Year, and such Meeting shall be on the first Monday in December, unless they shall by Law appoint a different Day.

Section 5. Each House shall be the Judge of the Elections, Returns, and Qualifications of its own Members, and a Majority of each shall constitute a Quorum to do Business, but a smaller Number may adjourn from day to day and may be authorized to compel the Attendance of absent Members, in such Manner, and under such Penalties as each House may provide.

Each House may determine the Rules of its Proceedings, punish its Members for disorderly Behavior, and, with the Concurrence of two-thirds, expel a Member.

Each House shall keep a Journal of its Proceedings, and from time to time publish the same, excepting such Parts as may in their Judgment require Secrecy; and the Yeas and Nays of the Members of either House on any question shall, at the Desire of one-fifth of those Present, be entered on the Journal.

Neither House, during the Session of Congress, shall, without the Consent of the other, adjourn for more than three days, nor to any other Place than that in which the two Houses shall be sitting.

Section 6. The Senators and Representatives shall receive a Compensation for their Services, to be ascertained by Law and paid out of the Treasury of the United States. They shall in all Cases, except Treason, Felony, and Breach of the Peace, be privileged from Arrest during their Attendance at the Session of their respective Houses, and in going to and returning from the same, and for any Speech or Debate in either House, they shall not be questioned in any other Place.

No Senator or Representative shall, during the Time for which he was elected, be appointed to any civil Office under the Authority of the United States, which shall have been created, or the Emoluments whereof shall have been increased during such time; and no Person holding any Office under the United States, shall be a Member of either House during his Continuance in Office.

Section 7. All Bills for raising Revenue shall originate in the House of Representatives, but the Senate may propose or concur with Amendments as on other Bills.

Every Bill which shall have passed the House of Representatives and the Senate shall, before it become a Law, be presented to the President of the United States. If he approve, he shall sign it, but if not, he shall return it, with his Objections to that House in which it shall have originated, who shall enter the Objections at large on their Journal and proceed to reconsider it. If after such Reconsideration, two-thirds of that House shall agree to pass the Bill, it shall be sent, together with the Objections, to the other House, by which it shall likewise be reconsidered, and if approved by two-thirds of that House, it shall become a Law. But in all such Cases, the Votes of both Houses shall be determined by yeas and Nays, and the Names of the Persons voting for and against the Bill shall be entered on the Journal of each House respectively. If any Bill shall not be returned by the President within ten days (Sundays excepted) after it shall have been presented to him, the Same shall be a Law, in like Manner as if he had signed it, unless the Congress by their Adjournment prevent its Return, in which Case it shall not be a Law.

Every Order, Resolution, or Vote to which the Concurrence of the Senate and House of Representatives may be necessary (except on a question of Adjournment) shall be presented to the President of the United States; and, before the Same shall take Effect, shall be approved by him, or being disapproved by him, shall be repassed by two-thirds of the Senate and House of Representatives, according to the Rules and Limitations prescribed in the Case of a Bill.

Section 8. The Congress shall have Power To lay and collect Taxes, Duties, Imposts, and Excises, to pay the Debts and provide for the common Defense and general Welfare of the United States; but all Duties, Imposts, and Excises shall be uniform throughout the United States;

To borrow Money on the credit of the United States;

To regulate Commerce with foreign Nations, and among the several States, and with the Indian Tribes;

To establish an uniform Rule of Naturalization, and uniform Laws on the subject of Bankruptcies throughout the United States;

To coin Money, regulate the Value thereof, and of foreign Coin, and fix the Standard of Weights and Measures;

To provide for the Punishment of counterfeiting the Securities and current Coin of the United States;

To establish Post Offices and post Roads;

To promote the Progress of Science and useful Arts by securing for limited Times to Authors and Inventors the exclusive Right to their respective Writings and Discoveries;

To constitute Tribunals inferior to the supreme Court;

To define and punish Piracies and Felonies committed on the high Seas and Offenses against the Law of Nations;

To declare War, grant Letters of Marque and Reprisal, and make Rules concerning Captures on Land and Water;

To raise and support Armies, but no Appropriation of Money to that Use shall be for a longer Term than two Years;

To provide and maintain a Navy;

To make Rules for the Government and Regulation of the land and naval Forces;

To provide for calling forth the Militia to execute the Laws of the Union, suppress Insurrections, and repel Invasions;

To provide for organizing, arming, and disciplining the Militia and for governing such Part of them as may be employed in the Service of the United States, reserving to the States respectively, the Appointment of the Officers, and the Authority of training the Militia according to the discipline prescribed by Congress;

To exercise exclusive Legislation in all Cases whatsoever, over such District (not exceeding ten Miles square) as may, by Cession of particular States and the Acceptance of Congress, become the Seat of the Government of the United States, and to exercise like Authority over all Places purchased by the Consent of the Legislature of the State in which the Same shall be, for the Erection of Forts, Magazines, Arsenals, dock- Yards, and other needful Buildings;—And o make all Laws which shall be necessary and proper for carrying into Execution the foregoing Powers, and all other Powers vested by this Constitution in the Government of the United States, or in any Department or Officer thereof.

Section 9. The Migration or Importation of such Persons as any of the States now existing shall think proper to admit shall not be prohibited by the Congress prior to the Year one thousand eight hundred and eight, but a Tax or duty may be imposed on such Importation, not exceeding ten dollars for each Person.

The Privilege of the Writ of Habeas Corpus shall not be suspended, unless when in Cases of Rebellion or Invasion the, public Safety may require it.

No Bill of Attainder or ex post facto Law shall be passed.

No Capitation, or other direct, Tax shall be laid, unless in Proportion to the Census or Enumeration herein before directed to be taken.

No Tax or Duty shall be laid on Articles exported from any State.

No Preference shall be given by any Regulation of Commerce or Revenue to the Ports of one State over those of another, nor shall Vessels bound to or from one State be obliged to enter, clear, or pay Duties in another.

No Money shall be drawn from the Treasury, but in Consequence of Appropriations made by Law, and a regular Statement and Account of the Receipts and Expenditures of all public Money shall be published from time to time.

No Title of Nobility shall be granted by the United States, And no Person holding any Office of Profit or Trust under them shall, without the Consent of the Congress, accept of any present, Emolument, Office, or Title of any kind, whatever, from any King, Prince, or foreign State.

Section 10. No State shall enter into any Treaty, Alliance, or Confederation; grant Letters of Marque and Reprisal; coin Money; emit Bills of Credit; make any Thing but gold and silver Coin a Tender in Payment of Debts; pass any Bill of Attainder, ex post facto Law, or Law impairing the Obligation of Contracts, or grant any Title of Nobility.

No State shall, without the Consent of the Congress, lay any Imposts or Duties on Imports or Exports, except what may be absolutely necessary for executing its inspection Laws: and the net Produce of all Duties and Imposts, laid by any State on Imports or Exports, shall be for the Use of the Treasury of the United States; and all such Laws shall be subject to the Revision and Control of the Congress.

No State shall, without the Consent of Congress, lay any Duty of Tonnage, keep Troops or Ships of War in time of Peace, enter into any Agreement or Compact with another State or with a foreign Power, or engage in War, unless actually invaded, or in such imminent Danger as will not admit of delay.

Article II

Section 1. The executive Power shall be vested in a President of the United States of America. He shall hold his Office during the Term of four Years and, together with the Vice President chosen for the same Term, be elected as follows:

Each State shall appoint, in such Manner as the Legislature thereof may direct, a Number of Electors, equal to the whole Number of Senators and Representatives to which the State may be entitled in the Congress: but no Senator or Representative, or Person holding an Office of Trust or Profit under the United States, shall be appointed an Elector.

The Electors shall meet in their respective States and vote by Ballot for two Persons, of whom one at least shall not be an Inhabitant of the same State with themselves. And they shall make a List of all the Persons voted for, and of the Number of Votes for each, which List they shall sign and certify, and transmit sealed to the Seat of the Government of the United States, directed to the President of the Senate. The President of the Senate shall, in the Presence of the Senate and House of Representatives, open all the Certificates, and the Votes shall be counted. The Person having the greatest Number of Votes shall be the President if such Number be a Majority of the whole Number of Electors appointed; and if there be more than one who have such Majority and have an equal Number of Votes, then the

House of Representatives shall immediately choose by Ballot one of them for President; and if no Person have a Majority, then from the five highest on the List the said House shall in like Manner choose the President. But in choosing the President, the Votes shall be taken by States, the Representation from each State having one Vote; a quorum for this Purpose shall consist of a Member or Members from two-thirds of the States, and a Majority of all the States shall be necessary to a Choice. In every Case, after the Choice of the President, the Person having the greatest Number of Votes of the Electors shall be the Vice President. But if there should remain two or more who have equal Votes, the Senate shall choose from them by Ballot the Vice President.

The Congress may determine the Time of choosing the Electors and the Day on which they shall give their Votes, which Day shall be the same throughout the United States.

No Person except a natural born Citizen or a Citizen of the United States at the time of the Adoption of this Constitution shall be eligible to the Office of President; neither shall any Person be eligible to that Office who shall not have attained to the Age of thirty-five Years, and been fourteen Years a Resident within the United States.

In Case of the Removal of the President from Office or of his Death, Resignation, or Inability to discharge the Powers and Duties of the said Office, the Same shall devolve on the Vice President, and the Congress may by Law provide for the Case of Removal, Death, Resignation or Inability, both of the President and Vice President, declaring what Officer shall then act as President, and such Officer shall act accordingly, until the Disability be removed, or a President shall be elected.

The President shall, at stated Times, receive for his Services a Compensation, which shall neither be increased nor diminished during the Period for which he shall have been elected, and he shall not receive within that Period any other Emolument from the United States or any of them.

Before he enters the Execution of his Office, he shall take the following Oath or Affirmation:—"I do solemnly swear (or affirm) that I will faithfully execute the Office of President of the United States, and will to the best of my Ability, preserve, protect and defend the Constitution of the United States."

Section 2. The President shall be Commander in Chief of the Army and Navy of the United States and of the Militia of the several States when called into the actual Service of the United States; he may require the Opinion, in writing, of the principal Officer in each of the executive Departments, upon any Subject relating to the Duties of their respective Offices, and he shall have Power to grant Reprieves and Pardons for Offences against the United States, except in Cases of Impeachment.

He shall have Power, by and with the Advice and Consent of the Senate, to make Treaties, provided two-thirds of the Senators present concur; and he shall nominate, and by and with the Advice and Consent of the Senate, shall appoint Ambassadors, other public Ministers and Consuls, Judges of the supreme Court, and all other Officers of the United States, whose Appointments are not herein otherwise provided for, and which shall be established by Law: but the Congress may by Law vest the Appointment of such inferior Officers, as they think proper, in the President alone, in the Courts of Law, or in the Heads of Departments.

The President shall have the Power to fill up all Vacancies that may happen during the Recess of the Senate by granting Commissions which shall expire at the End of their next Session.

Section 3. He shall, from time to time, give to the Congress Information of the State of the Union and recommend to their Consideration such Measures as he shall judge necessary and expedient; he may, on extraordinary Occasions, convene both Houses, or either of them, and in Case of Disagreement between them, with Respect to the Time of Adjournment, he may adjourn them to such Time as he shall think proper; he shall receive Ambassadors and other public Ministers; he shall take Care that the Laws be faithfully executed, and shall Commission all the Officers of the United States.

Section 4. The President, Vice President, and all civil Officers of the United States shall be removed from Office on Impeachment for, and Conviction of, Treason, Bribery, or other high Crimes and Misdemeanors.

Article III

Section 1. The judicial Power of the United States shall be vested in one supreme Court and in such inferior Courts as the Congress may from time to time ordain and establish.

The Judges, both of the supreme and inferior Courts, shall hold their Offices during good Behavior, and shall, at stated Times, receive for their Services, a Compensation, which shall not be diminished during their Continuance in Office.

Section 2. The judicial Power shall extend to all Cases, in Law and Equity, arising under this Constitution, the Laws of the United States, and Treaties made, or which shall be made, under their Authority;—to all Cases affecting Ambassadors, other public Ministers and Consuls;—to all Cases of admiralty and maritime Jurisdiction;—to Controversies to which the United States shall be a Party;—to Controversies between two or more States;—between a State and Citizens of another State; —between Citizens of different States, —between Citizens of the same State claiming Lands under Grants of different States, and between a State, or the Citizens thereof, and foreign States, Citizens or Subjects.

In all Cases affecting Ambassadors, other public Ministers and Consuls, and those in which a State shall be Party, the Supreme Court shall have original Jurisdiction. In all the other Cases before mentioned, the Supreme Court shall have appellate Jurisdiction, both as to Law and Fact, with such Exceptions and under such Regulations as the Congress shall make.

The Trial of all Crimes, except in Cases of Impeachment, shall be by Jury, and such Trial shall be held in the State where the said Crimes shall have been committed; but when not committed within any State, the Trial shall be at such Place or Places as the Congress may by Law have directed.

Section 3. Treason against the United States shall consist only in levying War against them or in adhering to their Enemies, giving them Aid and Comfort. No Person shall be convicted of Treason unless on the Testimony of two Witnesses to the same overt Act or on Confession in open Court. The Congress shall have Power to declare the Punishment of

Treason, but no Attainder of Treason shall work Corruption of Blood or Forfeiture except during the Life of the Person attainted.

Article IV

Section 1. Full Faith and Credit shall be given in each State to the public Acts, Records, and judicial Proceedings of every other State. And the Congress may by general Laws prescribe the Manner in which such Acts, Records and Proceedings shall be proved, and the Effect thereof.

Section 2. The Citizens of each State shall be entitled to all Privileges and Immunities of Citizens in the several States.

A Person charged in any State with Treason, Felony, or other Crime who shall flee from Justice and be found in another State shall, on Demand of the executive Authority of the State from which he fled, be delivered up, to be removed to the State having Jurisdiction of the Crime.

No Person held to Service or Labor in one State, under the Laws thereof, escaping into another, shall, in Consequence of any Law or Regulation therein, be discharged from such Service or Labor, but shall be delivered up on Claim of the Party to whom such Service or Labor may be due.

Section 3. New States may be admitted by the Congress into this Union, but no new State shall be formed or erected within the Jurisdiction of any other State; nor any State be formed by the Junction of two or more States, or Parts of States, without the Consent of the Legislatures of the States concerned as well as of the Congress.

The Congress shall have Power to dispose of and make all needful Rules and Regulations respecting the Territory or other Property belonging to the United States, and nothing in this Constitution shall be so construed as to Prejudice any Claims of the United States or of any particular State.

Section 4. The United States shall guarantee to every State in this Union a Republican Form of Government and shall protect each of them against Invasion and on Application of the Legislature or of the Executive (when the Legislature cannot be convened) against domestic Violence.

Article V

The Congress, whenever two-thirds of both Houses shall deem it necessary, shall propose Amendments to this Constitution, or, on the Application of the Legislatures of two-thirds of the several States, shall call a Convention for proposing Amendments, which, in either Case, shall be valid to all Intents and Purposes, as Part of this Constitution, when ratified by the Legislatures of three-fourths of the several States, or by Conventions in three fourths thereof, as the one or the other Mode of Ratification may be proposed by the Congress; Provided that no Amendment which may be made prior to the Year One thousand eight hundred and eight shall in any Manner affect the first and fourth Clauses in the Ninth Section of the first Article; and that no State, without its Consent, shall be deprived of its equal Suffrage in the Senate.

Article VI

All Debts contracted and Engagements entered into before the Adoption of this Constitution shall be as valid against the United States under this Constitution as under the Confederation. This Constitution, and the Laws of the United States which shall be made in Pursuance thereof; and all Treaties made, or which shall be made, under the Authority of the United States, shall be the supreme Law of the Land; and the Judges in every State shall be bound thereby, any Thing in the Constitution or Laws of any State to the Contrary notwithstanding.

The Senators and Representatives before mentioned, and the Members of the several State Legislatures, and all executive and judicial Officers, both of the United States and of the several States, shall be bound by Oath or Affirmation, to support this Constitution; but no religious Test shall ever be required as a Qualification to any Office or public Trust under the United States.

Article VII

The Ratification of the Conventions of nine States shall be sufficient for the Establishment of this Constitution between the States so ratifying the Same.

Done in Convention by the Unanimous Consent of the States present the Seventeenth Day of September in the Year of our Lord one thousand seven hundred and Eighty-seven and of the Independence of the United States of America the Twelfth In witness whereof We have hereunto subscribed our Names.

George Washington—

President and deputy from Virginia

Delaware

George Read, Gunning Bedford, Jr., John Dickinson, Richard Bassett, Jacob Broom

Maryland

James McHenry, Daniel of St. Thomas Jenifer, Daniel Carroll

Virginia

John Blair, James Madison Jr.

North Carolina

William Blount, Richard Dobbs Spaight, Hugh Williamson

South Carolina

John Rutledge, Charles Cotesworth Pinckney, Charles Pinckney, Pierce Butler

Georgia

William Few, Abraham Baldwin

New Hampshire

John Langdon, Nicholas Gilman

Massachusetts

Nathaniel Gorham, Rufus King

Connecticut

William Samuel Johnson, Roger Sherman

New York

Alexander Hamilton

New Jersey

> William Livingston, David Brearley, William Paterson, Jonathan Dayton

Pennsylvania

> Benjamin Franklin, Thomas Mifflin, Robert Morris, George Clymer, Thomas FitzSimmons, Jared Ingersoll, James Wilson, Gouverneur Morris

Attest William Jackson Secretary

The Bill of Rights

THE BILL OF RIGHTS AMENDMENTS 1 - 10

Congress OF THE United States
begun and held at the City of New York on Wednesday the fourth of
March, one thousand seven hundred and eighty-nine.

THE Conventions of a number of the States, having at the time of their adopting the Constitution, expressed a desire, in order to prevent misconstruction or abuse of its powers that further declaratory and restrictive clauses should be added: And as extending the ground of public confidence in the Government, will best ensure the beneficent ends of its institution.

RESOLVED by the Senate and House of Representatives of the United States of America, in Congress assembled, two-thirds of both Houses concurring, that the following Articles be proposed to the Legislatures of the several States as amendments to the Constitution of the United States, all, or any of which Articles, when ratified by three-fourths of the said Legislatures, to be valid to all intents and purposes, as part of the said Constitution; viz.

ARTICLES in addition to, and Amendment of the Constitution of the United States of America, proposed by Congress, and ratified by the Legislatures of the several States, pursuant to the fifth Article of the original Constitution.

(Articles I through X are known as the Bill of Rights) ratified Article the first. After the first enumeration required by the first Article of the Constitution, there shall be one Representative for every thirty thousand, until the number shall amount to one hundred, after which, the proportion shall be so regulated by Congress, that there shall be not less than one hundred Representatives, nor less than one Representative for every forty thousand persons until the number of Representatives shall amount to two hundred, after which the proportion shall be so regulated by Congress, that there shall not be less than two hundred Representatives, nor more than one Representative for every fifty thousand persons.

Article the second ..... No law, varying the compensation for the services of the Senators and Representatives, shall take effect until an election of Representatives shall have intervened. See Amendment XXVII

Amendment I (Freedom of religion and expression)
Ratified December 15, 1791

Congress shall make no law respecting an establishment of religion, or prohibiting the free exercise thereof, or abridging the freedom of speech, or of the press; or the right of the people peaceably to assemble, and to petition the Government for a redress of grievances.

Amendment II (Bearing Arms)
Ratified December 15, 1791

A well regulated Militia, being necessary to the security of a free State, the right of the people to keep and bear Arms, shall not be infringed.

Amendment III (Quartering Soldiers)
Ratified December 15, 1791

No Soldier shall, in time of peace, be quartered in any house without the consent of the Owner, nor in time of war, but in a manner to be prescribed by law.

Amendment IV (Search and Seizure)
Ratified December 15, 1791

The right of the people to be secure in their persons, houses, papers, and effects, against unreasonable searches and seizures, shall not be violated, and no Warrants shall issue, but upon probable cause, supported by Oath or affirmation, and particularly describing the place to be searched, and the persons or things to be seized.

Amendment V (Rights of Persons)
Ratified December 15, 1791

No person shall be held to answer for a capital or otherwise infamous crime, unless on a presentment or indictment of a Grand Jury, except in cases arising in the land or naval forces or in the Militia, when in actual service in time of War or public danger; nor shall any person be subject for the same offense to be twice put in jeopardy of life or limb; nor shall be compelled in any criminal case to be a witness against himself, nor be deprived of life, liberty, or property, without due process of law; nor shall private property be taken for public use, without just compensation.

Amendment VI (Rights of Accused in Criminal Prosecutions)
Ratified December 15, 1791

In all criminal prosecutions, the accused shall enjoy the right to a speedy and public trial by an impartial jury of the State and district wherein the crime shall have been committed, which district shall have been previously ascertained by law, and to be informed of the nature and cause of the accusation; to be confronted with the witnesses against him; to have compulsory process for obtaining witnesses in his favor, and to have the Assistance of Counsel for his defense.

Amendment VII (Civil Trials)
Ratified December 15, 1791

In Suits at common law, where the value in controversy shall exceed twenty dollars, the right of trial by jury shall be preserved, and no fact tried by a jury shall be otherwise re-examined in any Court of the United States than according to the rules of the common law.

Amendment VIII (Further Guarantees in Criminal Cases)
Ratified December 15, 1791

Excessive bail shall not be required, nor excessive fines imposed, nor cruel and unusual punishments inflicted.

Amendment IX (Unenumerated Rights)
Ratified December 15, 1791

The enumeration in the Constitution of certain rights shall not be construed to deny or disparage others retained by the people.

Amendment X (Reserved Powers)
Ratified December 15, 1791

The powers not delegated to the United States by the Constitution, nor prohibited by it to the States, are reserved to the States respectively or to the people.

Attest John Beckley, Clerk of the House of Representatives; Sam. A. Otis, Secretary of the Senate; Frederick Augustus Muhlenberg, Speaker of the House of Representatives; and John Adams, Vice President of the United States, and President of the Senate.

Amendments 11 – 27 to the U.S. Constitution

AMENDMENTS 11 - 27 to the U.S. CONSTITUTION

Amendment XI (Suits Against States)
Ratified February 7, 1795

The Judicial power of the United States shall not be construed to extend to any suit in law or equity commenced or prosecuted against one of the United States by Citizens of another State or by Citizens or Subjects of any Foreign State.

Amendment XII (Election of President)
Ratified June 15, 1804

The Electors shall meet in their respective states, and vote by ballot for President and Vice-President, one of whom, at least, shall not be an inhabitant of the same state with themselves; they shall name in their ballots the person voted for as President, and in distinct ballots the person voted for as Vice-President, and they shall make distinct lists of all persons voted for as President, and of all persons voted for as Vice- President, and of the number of votes for each, which lists they shall sign and certify, and transmit sealed to the seat of the government of the United States, directed to the President of the Senate;—the President of the Senate shall, in the presence of the Senate and House of Representatives, open all the certificates and the votes shall then be counted;—The person having the greatest number of votes for President, shall be the President, if such number be a majority of the whole number of Electors appointed; and if no person have such majority, then from the persons having the highest numbers not exceeding three on the list of those voted for as President, the House of Representatives shall choose immediately, by ballot, the President. But in choosing the President, the votes shall be taken by states, the representation from each state having one vote; a quorum for this purpose shall consist of a member or members from two-thirds of the states, and a majority of all the states shall be necessary to a choice. And if the House of Representatives shall not choose a President whenever the right of choice shall devolve upon them, before the fourth day of March next following, then the Vice-President shall act as President, as in the case of the death or other constitutional disability of the President. —The person having the greatest number of votes as Vice-President shall be the Vice-President if such number be a majority of the whole number of Electors appointed, and if no person has a majority, then from the two highest numbers on the list, the Senate shall choose the Vice-President; a quorum for the purpose shall consist of two-thirds of the whole number of Senators, and a majority of the whole number shall be necessary for a choice. But no person constitutionally ineligible to the office of President shall be eligible to that of Vice-President of the United States.

Amendment XIII (Slavery and Involuntary Servitude)
Ratified December 6, 1865

Section 1. Neither slavery nor involuntary servitude, except as a punishment for crime whereof the party shall have been duly convicted, shall exist within the United States or any place subject to their jurisdiction.

Section 2. Congress shall have power to enforce this article by appropriate legislation.

Amendment XIV (Rights Guaranteed: Privileges and Immunities of Citizenship, Due Process and Equal Protection)
Ratified July 9, 1868

Section 1. A persons born or naturalized in the United States and subject to the jurisdiction thereof are citizens of the United States and of the State wherein they reside. No State shall make or enforce any law which shall abridge the privileges or immunities of citizens of the United States; nor shall any State deprive any person of life, liberty, or property, without due process of law; nor deny to any person within its jurisdiction the equal protection of the laws.

Section 2. Representatives shall be apportioned among the several States according to their respective numbers, counting the whole number of persons in each State, excluding Indians not taxed. But when the right to vote at any election for the choice of electors for President and Vice President of the United States, Representatives in Congress, the Executive and Judicial officers of a State, or the members of the Legislature thereof, is denied to any of the male inhabitants of such State, being twenty-one years of age, and citizens of the United States, or in any way abridged, except for participation in rebellion, or other crime, the basis of representation therein shall be reduced in the proportion which the number of such male citizens shall bear to the whole number of male citizens twenty-one years of age in such State.

Section 3. No person shall be a Senator or Representative in Congress, or elector of President and Vice President, or hold any office, civil or military, under the United States, or under any State, who, having previously taken an oath, as a member of Congress, or as an officer of the United States, or as a member of any State legislature, or as an executive or judicial officer of any

State, to support the Constitution of the United States, shall have engaged in insurrection or rebellion against the same, or given aid or comfort to the enemies thereof. But Congress may, by a vote of two- thirds of each House, remove such disability.

Section 4. The validity of the public debt of the United States, authorized by law, including debts incurred for payment of pensions and bounties for services in suppressing insurrection or rebellion, shall not be questioned. But neither the United States nor any State shall assume or pay any debt or obligation incurred in aid of insurrection or rebellion against the United States, or any claim for the loss or emancipation of any slave; but all such debts, obligations, and claims shall be held illegal and void.

Section 5. The Congress shall have power to enforce, by appropriate legislation, the provisions of this article.

Amendment XV (Rights of Citizens to Vote)
Ratified February 3, 1870

Section 1. The right of citizens of the United States to vote shall not be denied or abridged by the United States or by any State on account of race, color, or previous condition of servitude.

Section 2. The Congress shall have power to enforce this article by appropriate legislation.

Amendment XVI (Income Tax)
Ratified February 3, 1913

The Congress shall have power to lay and collect taxes on incomes, from whatever source derived, without apportionment among the several States, and without regard to any census or enumeration.

Amendment XVII (Popular Election of Senators)
Ratified April 8, 1913

The Senate of the United States shall be composed of two Senators from each State, elected by the people thereof, for six years, and each Senator shall have one vote. The electors in each State shall have the qualifications requisite for electors of the most numerous branch of the State legislatures.

When vacancies happen in the representation of any State in the Senate, the executive authority of such State shall issue writs of election to fill such vacancies, *Provided* That the legislature of any State may empower the executive thereof to make temporary appointments until the people fill the vacancies by election as the legislature may direct. This amendment shall not be so construed as to affect the election or term of any Senator chosen before it becomes valid as part of the Constitution.

Amendment XVIII (Prohibition of Intoxicating Liquors)
Ratified January 16, 1919

Section 1. After one year from the ratification of this article the manufacture, sale, or transportation of intoxicating liquors within, the importation thereof into, or the exportation thereof from the United States and all territory subject to the jurisdiction thereof for beverage purposes is hereby prohibited.

Section 2: The Congress and the several States shall have concurrent power to enforce this article by appropriate legislation.

Section 3: This article shall be inoperative unless it shall have been ratified as an amendment to the Constitution by the legislatures of the several States, as provided in the Constitution, within seven years from the date of the submission hereof to the States by the Congress.

Amendment XIX (Women's Suffrage Rights)
Ratified August 18, 1920

The right of citizens of the United States to vote shall not be denied or abridged by the United States or by any State on account of sex. Congress shall have power to enforce this article by appropriate legislation.

Amendment XX (Terms of President, Vice President, Members of Congress: Presidential Vacancy)
Ratified January 23, 1933

Section 1. The terms of the President and Vice President shall end at noon on the 20th day of January, and the terms of Senators and Representatives at noon on the 3rd day of January, of the years in which such terms would have ended if this article had not been ratified, and the terms of their successors shall then begin.

Section 2: The Congress shall assemble at least once in every year, and such meeting shall begin at noon on the 3rd day of January unless they shall by law appoint a different day.

Section 3: If, at the time fixed for the beginning of the term of the President, the President elect shall have died, the Vice President elect shall become President. If a President shall not have been chosen before the time fixed for the beginning of his term, or if the president-elect shall have failed to qualify, then the Vice President elect shall act as President until a President shall have qualified, and the Congress may by law provide for the case wherein neither a President-elect nor a Vice President elect shall have qualified, declaring who shall then act as President, or the manner in which one who is to act shall be selected, and such person shall act accordingly until a President or Vice President shall have qualified.

Section 4: The Congress may by law provide for the case of the death of any of the persons from whom the House of Representatives may choose a President whenever the right of choice shall have devolved upon them, and for the case of the death of any of the persons from whom the Senate may choose a Vice President whenever the right of choice shall have devolved upon them.

Section 5: Sections 1 and 2 shall take effect on the 15th day of October following the ratification of this article.

Section 6: This article shall be inoperative unless it shall have been ratified as an amendment to the Constitution by the legislatures of three-fourths of the several States within seven years from the date of its submission.

Amendment XXI (Repeal of Eighteenth Amendment)
Ratified December 5, 1933

Section 1: The eighteenth article of amendment to the Constitution of the United States is hereby repealed.

Section 2: The transportation or importation into any State, Territory, or possession of the United States for delivery or use therein of intoxicating liquors, in violation of the laws thereof, is hereby prohibited.

Section 3: This article shall be inoperative unless it shall have been ratified as an amendment to the Constitution by conventions in the several States, as provided in the Constitution, within seven years from the date of the submission hereof to the States by the Congress.

Amendment XXII (Presidential Tenure)
Ratified February 27, 1951

Section 1. No person shall be elected to the office of the President more than twice, and no person who has held the office of President or acted as

President for more than two years of a term to which some other person was elected President shall be elected to the office of the President more than once. But this article shall not apply to any person holding the office of President when this article was proposed by the Congress and shall not prevent any person who may be holding the office of President, or acting as President, during the term within which this article becomes operative from holding the office of President or acting as President during the remainder of such term.

Section 2: This article shall be inoperative unless it shall have been ratified as an amendment to the Constitution by the legislatures of three-fourths of the several states within seven years from the date of its submission to the states by the Congress.

Amendment XXIII (Presidential Electors for the District of Columbia)
Ratified March 29, 1961

Section 1: The District constituting the seat of Government of the United States shall appoint in such manner as the Congress may direct:

A number of electors of President and Vice President equal to the whole number of Senators and Representatives in Congress to which the District would be entitled if it were a State, but in no event more than the least populous State; they shall be in addition to those appointed by the States, but they shall be considered, for the purposes of the election of President and Vice President, to be electors appointed by a state; and they shall meet in the District and perform such duties as provided by the twelfth article of amendment.

Section 2: The Congress shall have power to enforce this article by appropriate legislation.

Amendment XXIV (Abolition of the Poll Tax Qualification in Federal Elections)
Ratified January 23, 1964

Section 1. The right of citizens of the United States to vote in any primary or other election for President or Vice President, for electors for President or Vice President, or for Senator or Representative in Congress shall not be denied or abridged by the United States or any State by reason of failure to pay any poll tax or other tax.

Section 2. The Congress shall have power to enforce this article by appropriate legislation.

Amendment XXV (Presidential Vacancy, Disability, and Inability)
Ratified February 10, 1967

Section 1: In case of the removal of the President from office or of his death or resignation, the Vice President shall become President.

Section 2: Whenever there is a vacancy in the office of the Vice President, the President shall nominate a Vice President who shall take office upon confirmation by a majority vote of both Houses of Congress.

Section 3: Whenever the President transmits to the President pro tempore of the Senate and the Speaker of the House of Representatives his written declaration that he is unable to discharge the powers and duties of his office, and until he transmits to them a written declaration to the contrary, such powers and duties shall be discharged by the Vice President as Acting President.

Section 4: Whenever the Vice President and a majority of either the principal officers of the executive departments or of such other body as

Congress may by law provide, transmit to the President pro tempore of the Senate and the Speaker of the House of Representatives their written declaration that the President is unable to discharge the powers and duties of his office, the Vice President shall immediately assume the powers and duties of the office as Acting President.

Thereafter, when the President transmits to the President pro tempore of the Senate and the Speaker of the House of Representatives his written declaration that no inability exists, he shall resume the powers and duties of his office unless the Vice President and a majority of either the principal officers of the executive department or of such other body as Congress may by law provide, transmit within four days to the President pro tempore of the Senate and the Speaker of the House of Representatives their written declaration that the President is unable to discharge the powers and duties of his office. Thereupon, Congress shall decide the issue, assembling within forty-eight hours for that purpose if not in session. If the Congress, within twenty- one days after receipt of the latter written declaration, or if Congress is not in session, within twenty-one days after Congress is required to assemble, determines by two- thirds vote of both Houses that the President is unable to discharge the powers and duties of his office, the Vice President shall continue to discharge the same as Acting President; otherwise, the President shall resume the powers and duties of his office.

Amendment XXVI (Reduction of Voting Age Qualification)
Ratified July 1, 1971

Section 1: The right of citizens of the United States who are 18 years of age or older to vote shall not be denied or abridged by the United States or any state on account of age.

Section 2: The Congress shall have the power to enforce this article by appropriate legislation.

Amendment XXVII (Congressional Pay Limitation)
Ratified May 7, 1992

No law varying the compensation for the services of the Senators and Representatives shall take effect until an election of Representatives shall have intervened.

ABOUT THE AUTHOR

Joseph J. Ridgway is a New Jersey attorney who has practiced law for over forty-five years. Ridgway is a graduate of Seton Hall University, where he majored in psychology. He is also a graduate of Rutgers School of Law (JD) and Temple University School of Law (LLM in Taxation). Over the course of his legal and academic career as an adjunct instructor, Ridgway has taught American history, business law, and criminal law at various New Jersey and Pennsylvania colleges and universities.

In addition to writing children's literature historical fiction, Ridgway is an award-winning poet, being consistently nominated for numerous prestigious Pushcart Prizes for his stellar poetry. Further, the author is an accomplished essayist, with his writings appearing in a variety of nationwide publications.

Ridgway lives in Marlton, New Jersey, with his wife Diane and their rescue dog Sadie.

READER'S NOTES

_____

_____

_____

_____

_____

_____

_____

_____

_____

_____

_____

_____

_____

_____

_____

_____

_____

READER'S NOTES

READER'S NOTES

_____

_____

_____

_____

_____

_____

_____

_____

_____

_____

_____

_____

_____

_____

_____

_____

_____

_____